To Chris —

THE GREEN TSUNAMI

A Tidal Wave of Eco-Babble
Drowning Us All

Warren Duffy

Duffy Books

We want to hear from you. Please send your comments about this book to us in care of www.duffyandcompany.com. Thank you.

Duffy Books

The Green Tsunami
A Tidal Wave Of Eco-Babble Drowning Us All
Copyright © 2013 by Warren Duffy

This title is available in paperback at createspace.com
or as a Kindle ebook at Amazon.com

Requests for information should be addressed to:
Duffy Books, P.O. Box 1190, Huntington Beach, CA 92647
www.DuffyandCompany.com

The Library of Congress has cataloged the edition as follows:
ISBN-10: 1-482-67510-2
ISBN-13: 978-1-482-67510-8

Dedication

This book is dedicated to those who seek and stand for truth; and to those who recognize that our American inheritance is born of 2,000 years of martyr's blood and 200 years of patriot's dreams. May our generation not squander such a treasure.

Contents

Acknowledgements

First and foremost, this book would not be possible without the collaboration and support—wisdom and love—from my wife, Pam. Without her encouragement and steadfastness, you would not be holding this book in your hand.

Second, I express my gratitude to Darrel Trulson for the cover art, design and other great contributions. He took the concept from the drawing board to publication. You can contact Darrel at darrel-trulson@gmail.com

Third, to my many friends and colleagues, who have encouraged, helped and supported my journey along this path. To acknowledge them all by name is impossible but you know who you are and I thank you—each and all.

Finally, I thank my Irish parents—William and Nelly—who taught me to always stand up to bullies, no matter the cost.

Forward

I believe there are three great threats to America today. Any one of them could cause the demise of our nation and an end to the freedoms and way of life that was passed on to us centuries ago.

One such threat, and it tops the list, is **Islamic Terrorism**.

Strangely our government seems to be unwilling to admit, that in the name of a narrow interpretation of the Islamic religion, there are groups of individuals around the world and nation-states that have embraced the goal of imposing their beliefs on the rest of the world. Since 9-11, Al-Qaeda is one such Islamic Terrorist organization we have all come to know quite well. Unless we wake up now, as Islamic Terrorism spreads its tentacles around the world, the fear it creates, the death and destruction it causes, will soon overtake Western civilization. As a result of the "Arab Spring" and Egypt's election of a new president, "Sharia Law" is now the law of their land; however, for years it has been functioning in many other nations around the world. Should this movement spread through America, it will cost our nation dearly. We must recognize Islamic Terrorism as the great threat it is to America today.

The second threat operating within our borders is **Communism**.

Over the years, the term "communism" has been given the various labels of liberalism, progressivism, the "left" and socialism. Today these terms are virtually interchangeable because they all embrace a similar goal of an ever growing central government dictating to the rest of us how we must live our lives. The government will tell us what we can and cannot do and what we say and think. From this bloated government will flow expansive federal and state bureaucracies with endless costly programs adding to the nation's generational debt. This inflated size of government stifles an economy that once made America the most prosperous nation in the world. It not only controls us but saddles you, me, every American citizen and future generations with an annual tax bill that, to our fathers and forefathers, was unthinkable.

The third great threat, equally as destructive to America and our freedoms, is **Globalism**.

This threat has many labels as well; the New World Order, One World Government, Global Governance or a One World Economy. In the past, this threat was usually tossed onto the ash heap of conspiracy theories, but I contend this threat is operating completely in the open today. Over the last 40 plus years, "Globalism", under the banner of the United Nations, has crept into our society by creating a labyrinth of agencies and organizations actively functioning in every capitol city of every nation in the world. The march to global governance is propelled by a small group of people who believe they have all of the answers to all of the world's problems. Since 1970, their primary point of entry has been through **the environment**—"a global problem that requires a global solution". The desire of the globalists is to impose *their* will, *their* way of life and *their* view of how the universe is to function for the rest of us.

Marcus Cicero, the Roman philosopher, wrote: "Not to know what happened before you were born, that is to be...forever a child". If you were not yet born when the first Earth Day was held and the modern day global environmental movement began, this book will help you grow in a more factually based understanding of the global world around you. And, if you were part of the "Me Generation" of the 60s and 70s or just wondering why all the environmental hand wringing is happening, this book will provide details you may have never known or perhaps just never connected with the U.N.'s global agenda and today's environmental movement.

This book has been forty plus years in the making. The research and thoughts are mine, but every claim made in this book is verifiable by a simple click of your computer mouse and a search of the subjects via the internet.

The goal of my book is to **educate, motivate** and **activate** you. Consider it also a warning. A giant "Green Tsunami" is gathering power on the distant horizon. Once it crashes on America's shores, "Globalism", under the guise of modern day environmentalism, will sweep away our individual freedoms and drown our greatest inheritance, American liberty.

To save our nation from the threat of "Globalism", you must do your part. It is a significant part to play in saving the American Dream for your children, grandchildren and great grand children. If you consider yourself a true, American patriot, read on…this book was written just for you.

Warren Duffy
Huntington Beach, California
United States of America

*The only thing necessary for the triumph of evil
is for good men to do nothing."*

—*Edmund Burke*

CHAPTER 1

THE BEGINNINGS:
1970, THE FIRST EARTH DAY

A friend once told me, "Before you can connect the dots, you must first collect the dots." Connecting the dots of the Globalist Environmental Agenda is not an easy task, but the sorry state of our nation and world, complex as it is, suddenly becomes much clearer once all the dots are collected and connected.

How has mankind been convinced that Planet Earth is in grave jeopardy because of the advances of the Industrial Age? This is the era of man's history that has given us so many incredible discoveries in manufacturing, transportation, communication, science and an extended life expectancy beyond anything man ever imagined possible. Is that time period now really causing our planet's imminent demise?

To answer that question and to collect and connect the dots is to retrace a 40 plus year journey that began quite innocently in 1970 and has evolved into a web of international intrigue and cast of incredibly diverse and sometimes rather loony characters. But, with the help of a willing global media, a handful of culpable globalists have convinced the world that a series of almost laughable, impending disasters are actually about to happen.

Let us begin collecting the dots by tracing the history of the very first Earth Day in the spring of 1970.

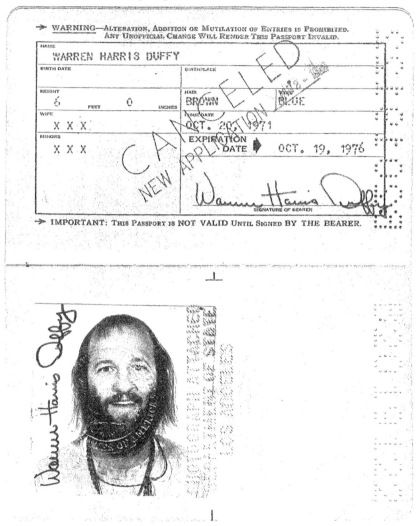

In the late 60s, the man in the above photograph was the Program Director of an "underground" radio station in Los Angeles, California known as "the Mighty Met", KMET-FM. That man was me. I headed a small group of committed hippies who all loved music; cutting edge, hard rock, underground music. The Who, Traffic, Led Zeppelin, Pink Floyd, Crosby, Stills, Nash and Young, Dr. John the Night Tripper, Joe Cocker, The Rolling Stones, The Beatles, Jimi Hendrix, Janis Joplin and Jim Morrison were all included on our daily play list.

In those heady days, part of being an underground radio station was to be a very active component in the "counter culture" movement, a younger group devoted to a new way of living that was the antithesis of our parent's materialistic, post-World War II generation. The goal in life wasn't a house in the suburbs with two cars in the driveway and a TV in the living room. Our generation wanted "Peace, Love, Flowers and Beads". We created alternative lifestyles and gathered together in small communities in out of the way places like the Haight-Ashbury District in San Francisco or the East Village in New York City.

We had an "underground" system of communication to help organize demonstrations against the Viet Nam War, "love-ins" and music festivals (Woodstock on the East Coast or the Altamont Rolling Stones concert on the West coast), while we "got high with a little help from our friends". Our clothing was somewhat mismatched and we went barefoot most of the time.

At the beach, we sprinted across the sand to the beautiful Pacific Ocean invariably stepping on discarded pieces of metal from soda and beer cans known as "pop tops". Jimmy Buffett summed up our mutual predicament of those days in his "Margaritaville" classic, "Took off my flip flop, stepped on a pop top—cut my foot had to hobble back home…."

All of those elements, simplistic, though they may have been, contributed to the fertile soil for the first "Earth Day".

During this same time period, an agile L.A. newspaper reporter observing the poor condition of L.A. air combined two elements clouding the skies, "smoke" and "fog", to create the word "smog". That expression soon became a favorite joke among late night television comedians, "Los Angeles, the city where you can see the air you breathe".

As a side note; do you know how "smog" was cured in the City of Angels? In the 1970s, someone invented the Catalytic Converter. It was a relatively simple car repair that cost little to install and fixed the problem of fumes leaking into the L.A. skies. In 1977, L.A. reported one hundred and twenty-one Stage One Smog Alerts. Since then, there have been none, zero—zip—nada—not one, Stage One Smog Alert.

In the late 60's, Los Angeles was not the only city in America dealing with foul air. Sadly, industrial pollution was also a serious problem for municipalities across the country. As giant steel mills belched smoke and cinders on Pittsburgh, Pennsylvania, it became yet another American town experiencing serious air pollution problems.

There were other environmental problems back then as well. In Southern California, a massive Santa Barbara Oil Spill of 1969 fouled our beaches, our fish, and our birds with slime and goo. Admittedly, though it was not as bad as the oil spill of 2009 off the Louisiana Gulf Coast or the Exxon Valdez oil spill in Alaska, it was, nonetheless, a significant event. The new "Surf Culture" was taking hold in Southern California and oil was washing onto the golden sands of its beaches.

In Ohio, the Cuyahoga River was so polluted with industrial waste it actually caught fire and burned for two days. Among the television pictures of 1969 was a river burning in Ohio, soot darkening the skies of Pittsburgh, smog blanketing the L.A. Basin, and the beaches of California polluted with oil. America was ripe for a more thoughtful approach of caring for the environment.

The youthful generation of "under-30-somethings" was ready to pledge ourselves to a new way of thinking about pollution. It was time to start leaving the camp site in better shape than we found it. No longer would we tolerate cigarette butts or litter being thrown out of car windows. We were committed to no smog, no water pollution and above all, no pop tops discarded on the beaches.

We resurrected an old biological word, "ecology" and branded our new crusade "The Ecology Movement", a word most people over 30 didn't even know how to pronounce.

Then an unlikely champion for our cause appeared in Washington, D.C. His name was Senator Gaylord Nelson from Wisconsin who organized a nationwide ecology "teach in" day that fit perfectly with the counter-culture crusade of the 60s. Senator Nelson named the big event "Earth Day"; in part because it sounded like 'birthday' that, in turn, sounded like a nationwide party. As news about the big event spread, the Senator encouraged local celebrations. Our counter culture radio station took the bait and organized Southern California's celebration of the first "Earth Day" on April 22, 1970.

As the much-anticipated day dawned, our listeners dutifully took their trash bags to tidy up the beach, giving extra attention to those irritating "pop tops" buried in the sand. We wagged our fingers at drivers who tossed litter from their car, cleaned up trash along the waterline and went to parks removing litter from parking lots and walking paths.

At the end of the day, we returned home feeling wonderful about our day long event. After inhaling suitable refreshments, we turned on the television news to watch the national news coverage of the big "Earth Day" celebration. Our collective jaws dropped as we saw and heard the network news from Chet Huntley and David Brinkley and the beloved CBS anchor, Walter Cronkite.

First, from Washington, D.C. our super-hero Senator Nelson appeared in a blazer, shirt and tie and spoke passionately to the crowd in our nation's capitol. Imagine my bewilderment when the Senator began his speech with a warning that mass extinctions on the planet were about to happen because of a coming environmental catastrophe. The Senator announced, "Doctor S. Dillon Ripley, Secretary of the Smithsonian Institute, believes that in 25 years 75% to 80% of all the species of living animals will be extinct."

Really? Smog was going to cause massive extinctions? The fate of our planet would be decided by people who tossed cigarette butts out of their car windows or "pop tops" in the sand at the beach? I was a shocked and surprised counter-culturist!

The news coverage then moved to a huge Earth Day event on Fifth Avenue in New York City. Here, a well-known biologist, Paul Ehrlich, author of the best selling book "The Population Bomb", was addressing the crowd. Ehrlich made no mention of "pop tops", nothing about cleaning up trash or keeping rivers and streams clean.

Instead he passionately expressed, "Populations will inevitably and completely outstrip whatever small increase in food supplies we make.

The death rate will increase until at least 100 to 200 million people per year will be starving to death in the next ten years." **Many years later, Ehrlich wrote the foreword to Al Gore's scary, environmental, blockbuster book, "Earth in the Balance".**

In 1970, Ken Watt was perhaps the best known and most respected environmental activist of the era. Shortly after the first "Earth Day, he made his "global environmental" claim that I think you will find humorous. "The world has been chilling sharply for about 20 years. If present trends continue the world will be about 4 degrees cooler for global mean temperatures in 1990, but 11 degrees colder in the year 2000. This is about twice what it would take to put us in an Ice Age."

It turns out all those gloomy predictions at the 1970 "Earth Day" were the genesis of the doomsday prophesies that continue today. From Watt's "Ice Age" to the latest prediction that "Global Warming" caused by greenhouse gases trapped in the Earth's atmosphere are resulting in "Climate Change", the list of imaginary disasters is continually perpetuated and yet to date, *not one,* has ever happened.

The television news coverage of America's first "Earth Day" ended and the networks returned to reporting about the ongoing Vietnam War, the trial of the demonstrators who disrupted the Chicago Democratic National Convention and the incredible news about America's brave Apollo 13 astronauts. The following day we arrived at the radio studio to compare notes and agreed; the organizers of "Earth Day" were obviously pursuing an agenda for this "new environmental movement" with national and international implications most of us never imagined.

Enter the United Nations (U.N.). In 1971, within a year of the first Earth Day, this organization picked up the environmental flag and organized the first "International Earth Day". "Pollution is an international problem that requires an international solution", they claimed. After all, smoke from an industrial smoke stack in Mexico doesn't stop at the U.S. border. Once that smoke gets caught in the jet-stream, it is capable of depositing pollution anywhere in the world. The U.N. stressed that the nations of the world must join together in the new global environmental movement to clean up the debris of modern-day industrial pollution. And to accomplish that task, no matter what the cost, everyone on this planet must cooperate.

So, we have collected a few of the first dots in our quest to discern how the simple celebration of the first "Earth Day" by America's counter culture evolved into the environmental agenda of today. Over the past 40 plus years, there has been quite a metamorphosis.

Up until 2009, the United Nations had become the biggest promoter of the "Global Environmental Movement". It was then they decided to very quietly change the name of their International Earth Day celebration to "International Mother Earth Day". Any old counter-culturist will tell you, Mother Earth is a code name for the worship of the goddess Gaia, a strange subterranean cult that reverences the mythical goddess of creation. Today, at this annual U.N. celebration, they begin by honoring the goddess Gaia with the beating of Native American drums, the chants of Buddhist holy men, the pipe playing of Asian musicians and the dances of African tribes. All of that would strike a happy chord for us counter-culturists of the 60s and 70s. We loved Buddhist meditation, embraced African folk dancing and beautiful Asian pipe music. And though we liked Ravi Shankar's sitar music, Mother Earth and the goddess Gaia were a bit much for our crowd.

In the early 70s, we gave up life in the crowded and polluted cities of America and became "back to the earthers". We formed communes throughout America, with some very large ones in Tennessee and Kentucky. Voluntarily, we wanted to live close to nature and unplug from the constant drone of advanced civilization. But today, the new environmental movement does not embrace those desires in the same way.

Today's global environmentalists are *demanding* the global population (especially the voracious American consumers) to leave the rural lands, return to the cities, walk, ride bikes or use public transportation to lower our dependency on fossil fuel. We must depend on windmills and solar panels to keep our complex civilization moving forward. We must all learn to live like the Amish and return to a much simpler lifestyle.

The global elitists proclaim none of us need live in a power-gobbling, 2500 square foot private home. If we are truly environmentally conscious, we can pare down to an 800 square foot apartment, one stacked on top of the other, and all located within walking distance of a nearby public transportation stop. By doing all of this, (we are assured by the smirking new environmentalists), life will be good.

In fact, as this environmental movement has advanced into the new century, the economy, especially in California where my wife and I live, has turned very badly.

"Environmentally sensitive" politicians and venture capitalists learned there were huge profits to be made in a wide variety of California's "green energy" schemes. Windmills were among the first to be introduced, but these mammoth, garish skeletons of steel, fiberglass, and cast iron have not only tainted the pristine beauty of the land, but are found to be massive bird killers that includes hundreds of the Gold and Bald eagle species.

Today, the California deserts, once off limits to any kind of development and patrolled by armed agents of the federal Bureau of Land Management, are home to massive solar power plants. When seen close up, the size and scope of these gargantuan solar plant operations boggle the mind.

As aggressively and environmentally sensitive was the government's search for ways to replace fossil fuels and reduce air pollution, there began bio-fuel experiments of adding ethanol to gasoline. However like so many government programs, the "law of unintended consequences" soon raised its nasty head. The new ethanol was made from corn, corn that could have otherwise been used in the food supply. Perhaps, the most under-reported news story of the 1990s was the "tortilla riot" in Mexico. Here folks took to the streets protesting the high price of corn tortillas; still the basic food staple for the majority of Mexicans.

After investing billions of government dollars, corn ethanol was quietly abandoned in California to create new ethanol made from the stalks of sugar beets. Unfortunately, California doesn't produce enough beet sugar for the 27 million vehicles registered in the state, but the state government had a solution. They can **purchase and import** beet sugar stalks directly from Brazil! Did you get that?

In order to produce the "new" ethanol for their new grade of gasoline, California will redistribute our wealth to our neighbors in Brazil so we can buy beet sugar stalks and clean up those pesky greenhouse gases and solve the problem of "Global Warming". It is indeed interesting that as state and federal bureaucrats dried up California's lush farmlands by diverting water to save a tiny fish, the "Delta smelt"(that, according to radical environmentalists, was near extinction), they have taken away the livelihood of local farmers and workers who could have provided the very beet sugar our state is now outsourcing to Brazil.

As our dots connect, you must admit, they make perfect *nonsense*.

Consider President Barack Obama's Economic Stimulus package introduced almost 40 years after the first Earth Day. It underwrote dozens of those pipe-dream, green-energy and supposedly green-job-producing projects that many, after a few short years, have gone bankrupt.

We are now left to wonder, in a world supposedly so sophisticated and well informed by the incredible advances in information technology, how could all of this happen? How could the world fall for a litany of nonsensical, environmental about-to-happen catastrophes? How could we be convinced that some nifty computer projections could somehow accurately forecast the weather for the next hundred years? How could we be convinced to dramatically change the way we live, all in the name of saving the planet? How could a seemingly gullible international media simply ignore scientific analysis that says any theory must be reproduced in a laboratory under controlled conditions before we can accept it as being true?

Like me, you probably watch the local weather forecast on the nightly news. Often, the weather personality is the comic relief between the news and sports as he or she explains, in front of their "green board", those confusing high and low pressure systems that will dominate our local weather patterns for the next 5 or 7 days. We are warned of a coming storm, put on "Storm Alert" and told to fill the sand bags, stock up on water and buy extra batteries. Then the storm limps through, nothing much happens and the embarrassed weather forecaster tries to explain the storm simply did not materialize as predicted.

Now, compare that scenario to the crazy world of environmentalism. We are told by a cadre of supposedly world-class scientists, relying on nothing but 'garbage in-garbage out' computer models, they can predict what the weather will be like not only in our local communities, but in the entire universe for the next 90 years! Weather forecasters can't accurately predict a storm for tomorrow, but environmental science can predict weather from 2012 to 2099?

The mainstream media bought into the environmental agenda years ago and they have successfully convinced a gullible public that "the science is settled". Any scientist worthy of his white lab coat and "pocket protector" will tell you, "The science is never settled." Scientific theory is constantly scrutinized by even some of the theories we accepted long ago as true. One great example is Einstein's Theory of Relativity. His theory was tested and eventually corrected because it contained a bit of faulty math.

Domestically, the new environmental "alarmism" began with President Nixon's Clean Air Act of 1972. From this legislation, a monstrous new federal bureaucracy was created known as the Environmental Protection Agency (EPA). Among many environmentally driven projects, the agency created a list of "Endangered Species" that were threatened with extinction if not protected by law.

The list expanded greatly from the 1970s when saving the wolves and whales was our foremost concern. When the "Snail Darter" was added to the list, many began to wonder what the EPA was really protecting. Today, the "Endangered Species" list includes 10,801 names beginning with the Abbot's Boobie to the final entry the Zuniga Dark Rice Rat.

The EPA also regulated the Federal Government's oversight for the protection of a list of "endangered" wetlands, once called swamps. Next came the "Environmental Impact Reports" (EIR's) demanding before any construction project began on public or private land, the impact on "Nature" had to be investigated with particular emphasis on protecting "Endangered Species". Once the burdensome paperwork was filed with the government, an environmental organization would hire attorneys to file lawsuits that delayed building projects for years.

To the environmentalists of today, nothing is sacred, not even our light bulbs. The "Green Tsunami" creators have convinced the federal government that the old and inexpensive light bulbs must be replaced by new, expensive, "environmentally friendly" light bulbs made in Mexico. "Out with the old and in with the new", at any cost, is the environmental tidal wave of the future.

The federal, state, county and local government will fix all of our environmental problems by simply taking charge of all of our energy, the way we live, the way we travel and the way we illuminate our homes. And no one dare object to their environmental agenda lest they be labeled a "deny-er" or a "flat earth-er", or an "obstruction-ist", a "simpleton" or worse.

But today as these new environmental programs are gaining ground, many are taking a second look and reconsidering all they've been told the past four decades. They are revisiting the claims of impending disasters and the long list of proposed government solutions to regu-late their lives. For those of us who were there for that very first and very innocent, "Earth Day", the environmental movement has cer-tainly come a very long and frightening way.

CHAPTER 2

THE UNITED NATIONS:
A WORLD BODY SEEKS A CAUSE

As I alluded to in the last chapter, the driving force behind the new environmental movement is the United Nations, the organization that developed historically as a natural outgrowth from Word War II. After so many had died in combat and President Harry Truman ordered the release of the atom bomb to end the war in the Pacific, the threat of a "mushroom cloud" hovering over an American or European city was enough to motivate the post-war generation to create a new international organization to replace the non-functioning League of Nations. Theoretically, as long as there was a forum for peace operating somewhere in the world, mankind would never again choose war.

The words "United Nations" were first used by President Franklin Roosevelt on January 1, 1942, as a united pledge by world governments to continue the battle against the three major WWII enemies Germany, Italy and Japan. In 1945, representatives from 50 nations gathered in San Francisco to draw up a United Nations Charter that was ratified and signed by a majority of world countries. The United Nations first convened on January 10, 1946, but the idealism of the world's peace-niks was quickly shattered by the reality of the U.N.'s first major international crisis.

At midnight on May 14, 1948, the Provisional Government of Israel proclaimed the new State of Israel as a homeland for Jews who had been the target of Nazi extermination during WWII. Just twenty-four hours after Israel had been declared an independent country, neighboring Arab nations that objected to U.N. recognition of the fledgling Israeli state, invaded the country without warning. The U.N. was powerless to stop the warfare that spilled across international borders.

Two years later, June 25, 1950, a Korean civil war began. Five days later, United States ground forces were dispatched to stop the Chinese-backed north from over running the democracy in the south. Instead of restoring the peace, the U.N. recruited an army from the nations of the world to fight the Communist invaders, ironically calling them the "Peacekeepers".

In 1960, a controversial debate involving Russian dictator, Nikita Khrushchev, disrupted the annual gathering of the U.N. General Assembly by the ruler's unrelenting and contemptuous thumping of his shoe on the table in front of him. Since then, a steady stream of dictators and political malcontents have marched to the podium in the great marble hall of the New York City headquarters to rant and rave, usually spewing insults to the United States and/or Israel, while drawing standing ovations from many of the U.N. members.

When the U.N. became aware of a complicated and divisive war in Vietnam, they chose to remain unengaged. It began less than a week after Japan surrendered to end World War II. Communist guerilla leader Ho Chi Minh led an uprising that threatened the stability of the French colony in Indo China. France flew a body of well trained paratroopers into battle to end the rebellion; however, the conflict grew until finally the Chinese government sent troops and weapons to support Ho's revolt. Under President Kennedy, the United States joined the fighting (first as "advisors"), until young Americans were later drafted into military service and ordered into a warzone to fight the communist invasion of South Vietnam. As the war raged on and intensified, it became more unpopular with Americans back home.

Finally in 1973, the last contingency of American troops was withdrawn. Two years later, the President of South Vietnam proclaimed the national surrender to the Northern Communist Regime and again, the U.N. sat idly by, ineffective.

Various and assorted other "hot spots" continued to erupt around the world. There was outbreak between tribes in Africa, fighting among white settlers in South Africa and the native population to end "apartheid". In South America, communist dictators rose up, ran their course in office, then were overthrown by bloody rebellions. Once again the U.N. offered little help.

Perhaps the most dangerous threat to global stability came in the early 1960s when the two major powers of the world stood toe to toe, ready to slug it out in a nuclear confrontation. When Russia military bases were established in Cuba, complete with missiles that could easily reach the U.S. mainland, America president, John F. Kennedy, confronted the possibility of a nuclear war. The U.N. did nothing to help.

Obviously, keeping Global Peace was a United Nations failure. It was necessary the organization seek a single, global, unifying issue to validate their existence.

First, they tried Women's Rights, but one third of the member nations do not believe women have fundamental rights. Then the concept for the U.N. to eradicate colonialism was introduced. But colonial powers like Britain and France were already in the process of ending colonial rule, leaving the U.N. once again impotent.

Freedom of the Press was another issue proposed, but one opposed by dictators that firmly believed in a controlled media. Migrants' issues were suggested and the idea went nowhere. Abolition of slavery was introduced as early as 1949, yet, sex slavery continues more than six decades later and, in many cultures, children are treated as family slaves and begin working at a very young age to support their family.

Finally, one issue emerged that offered global government possibilities—a "new environmental movement" led by a feminist-socialist from Norway, Dr. Gro Harlem Brundtland. After studying medicine at Harvard, she returned home and became a physician in the state-run health care system. When the U.N. staged its first International

Earth Day in 1971, Dr. Brundtland was appointed to a newly created post in the Norwegian government and became the country's first Minister of Environmental Affairs. Dr. Brundtland's political philosophy emerged simultaneously when she was elected as vice president of Socialist International. Her career in politics blossomed and she was eventually elected not once, but twice, to serve the people of Norway as their Prime Minister.

Dr. Brundtland became an international force to be reckoned with and an extremely powerful player on the world stage. She convinced the Secretary-General of the United Nations, Javier Perez de Cuellar, to establish a new U.N. organization, "The World Commission on the Environment and Development". So powerful was her personal leadership, the new commission became known internationally as "The Brundtland Commission".

With an international U.N. team behind her, Dr. Brundtland created what was perhaps the most influential environmental document of the 1980s, one that would set the agenda for the U.N.'s new international environmental movement. The 415-page report titled "Our Common Future" not only outlined a global assault on many of the world's major health problems, but for the first time included environmental issues as an international cause for health concerns.

The complex, new document laid the groundwork for the first comprehensive United Nation's "Earth Summit" held in Rio de Janeiro, Brazil in 1992, chaired by Dr. Brundtland's long time cohort of her Brundtland Commission, Canadian businessman Maurice Strong. After serving as the Chairman of the Board of a large oil conglomerate, Petro-Canada, Strong became a very wealthy man. Brundtland and U.N. Secretary-General Cuellar appointed Strong to serve concurrently as Under-Secretary General of the entire U.N. global organization and to the post of Special Advisor to the Secretary General.

Strong combined his new global status, his friendship with Bruntland and his belief in the U.N. as a global organization to create the foundation for programs using environmental issues as the international problem that needed a peaceful U.N. solution. As Strong's personal wealth continued to grow, he and wife, Hanna, bought a large country estate in Vermont they named "Shelburne Farms". The family retreat was not far from the U.N. offices in New York City which also gave Hanna a perfect gathering spot for her "New Age" friends.

Hanna Strong was fond of meditating and chanting to her favorite goddess Maia (remember, that goddess of the earth's creation). Just before her husband banged his gavel and called the 1992 Earth Summit to order in Brazil, Hanna held a three-week vigil at the family farm where she introduced her newly minted creation called, "The Sacred Earth Charter". After she read it to those assembled, she buried the scroll on the property in something called "The Ark of Hope". Those present described the Charter as the "Magna Carta" of the people of the earth. One can only imagine how closely this document resembled the body of work created a few weeks later by the United Nation's Earth Summit. The scale of Hanna's big event can best be understood when it was later learned her special guest to begin the vigil was the Dalai Lama of Tibet, one of her hubby's old pals from the early days of his U.N. career.

As Secretary General of the U.N.'s 1992 Earth's Summit in Rio, Maurice Strong's opening remarks quite candidly expressed the intentions of the U.N.'s global environmentalism agenda. "Industrialized countries have developed and benefitted from the unsustainable patterns of production and consumption which have produced our current dilemma. It is clear that current lifestyle and consumption patterns of the affluent middle class, involving high meat intake, use of fossil fuels, appliances, home and work-place air conditioning and heating and suburban housing, are not sustainable. A shift is necessary toward lifestyles less geared to environmentally damaging consumption patterns."

"Sustainable" was a relatively new global environmental term in 1992, but can now be traced to one of the dots we collected earlier, The Brundtland Commission's "Our Common Future" report. "Sustainable", used throughout the 415-page report, quickly became the key code-word of the new global environmental movement.

To those from the counter-culture of the 60s and 70s, Strong's words seemed an attack. Many were already vegetarians, a choice for them that had nothing to do with a "sustainable" lifestyle to save Planet Earth. To those somewhat drug-compromised minds, frankly, eating meat seemed, well, cannibalistic. Also, during those days of anti-Viet Nam war protests, many drove Volkswagens to the big events. Was this new environmental movement being championed by the U.N. declaring war on their major form of transportation operated by fossil fuels? Riding a bike to a protest rally seemed like so much of a... well, a hassle. Was this counter culture that had rejected the values of "middle class" America from the 50s to 70s, now being lumped together as the enemy of the very environmental movement they started?

At the '92 Earth Summit, Strong also introduced a new socialist concept he called, "Social Justice" that soon morphed into "Environmental Justice". Whenever referenced at subsequent U.N. meetings, "social and environmental justice" included such blatantly socialist concepts as the abolition of private property, private transportation and the elimination of private farms in favor of "collectives". But the element most shocking to everyone was an emphasis on population control, a concept that harkened back to Paul Ehrlich's previously mentioned book, "The Population Bomb". This new position of the global environmentalist movement was to control the growth of the earth's population lest we over-populate the planet and are unable to "sustain" life (yet another reference to the new global goal of "sustainability"). Just how and what methods of control were they suggesting?

When asked to explain in more detail exactly what his concept of population control might look like in practical terms, Strong told a reporter, "Licenses to have babies, incidentally, is something that I got in trouble for some years ago for suggesting even in Canada that this might be necessary at some point, at least some restriction on the right to have a child."

In another interview prior to the opening of the U.N.'s Earth Summit, Strong explained his fundamental belief in global government as, "The right and opportunity of all people to benefit equally from the resources afforded us by society and the environment would be accomplished by the socialist/communist redistribution of wealth."

As I read those words in the 1990s, I recalled the writings of Karl Marx in 1875, "From each according to his abilities, to each according to his needs."

Surely, no American would embrace this new approach to a global environmental agenda with licenses to have babies and the redistribution of wealth so the rich would support the poor or, as America's first black President would later say, "We have to spread the wealth around a little".

That old counter-culture of the 60s and 70s might not have agreed with American foreign policy, but we all strongly believed in American freedom; freedom of conscience, freedom to explore new ideas, freedom to live as an individual, to live wherever you wanted and to pursue your dreams, no matter where they might take you. That fundamental vision of American Freedom was obviously diametrically opposite to the goals of the new U.N. "Global Environmentalism Movement." The more we have learned about it over the years, the more our fears have been confirmed.

Maurice Strong, by the way, has now abandoned America and established his 21st century life in a new part of the world. He and Hanna did not return to the sprawling farm in New England where the "ark" is buried, or to native Canada. They did not even move to Tokyo where Strong serves as President of the United Nation's University, the school that trains the next generation of U.N. global leaders. The couple now resides in the Peoples Republic of China in a compound of wealthy ex-pats. Mr. Strong's speaking appearances are growing much less frequent as he advances in age, with his last much-anticipated talk in San Francisco cancelled at the last minute sending along regrets with an explanation of being "very busy with projects in China".

Meanwhile back at the U.N.'s June, 1992 Earth Summit in Rio, the meeting was preparing to adjourn and delegates including President George H.W. Bush, who at one time served as the U.S. Ambassador to the U.N., signed a commitment to codify the new global environmental agenda as articulated by Strong and Brundtland. The new document would create a list of goals to be accomplished in the coming 21st century. Five years later, in 1997, that document was ratified at a U.N. follow-up environmental conference in Kyoto, Japan. **"The Agenda for the 21st Century" was born, now known as "Agenda 21".**

Though President H.W. Bush signed on to the commitment to the new environmental agenda, his defeat for re-election in 1992 did not permit him to carry out the obligation. However, with the election of Bill Clinton and Al Gore, this key environmental task was accomplished bypassing Congress. **On June 29, 1993, President Clinton signed Executive Order, #12852 creating the "President's Council on Sustainable Development".** Al Gore, who had already published his environmental best seller "Earth in the Balance", was named to head the new council. When the names of members were published a few months later, it included the leaders of some of the world's most aggressive global environmental organizations which we shall discuss in more detail a bit later.

According to "Agenda 21", the earth's "unsustainability" was being dramatically threatened by seven gases that previously seemed perfectly harmless to scientists everywhere. These so-called Greenhouse Gases (GHG's), now listed one by one in the Kyoto Accord and "Agenda 21", created the latest dire threat to the planet, "Global Warming". What a far cry from the "Ice Age" predicted at the first "Earth Day" in 1970.

Now let's identify those nasty greenhouse gases (GHG's).

The first is Carbon Dioxide (CO-2), a gas generated in greenhouses to make plants grow more abundantly. According to "Agenda 21", carbon dioxide is the single largest threat to mankind. Lest CO-2 warm the planet and create mayhem in the universe, carbon dioxide must be controlled by a cooperative Global Government campaign at virtually any cost.

The next gas is Methane. This is the gas produced in a mammal's digestive system. Cows became the radical environmentalists "bulls-eye" (excuse the pun) and the manure piles on the world's farms were labeled a threat to the future of mankind and the planet. Before long there would be no more "California Happy Cows".

The third gas, Nitrous Oxide, is the one dentists use to ease patient's anxiety during dental work. It is also known as "laughing gas". N2O was no laughing matter to the environmentalists. Those three gases, plus four others (with long scientific names I can't remember or pronounce), were supposedly combining to put Planet Earth into imminent peril unless the U.N. did something to control all of them.

The second "global goal" of the U.N.'s "Agenda 21" program seemed completely unrealistic. All nations of the world must agree voluntarily to roll back their pollution levels to where they were in 1990. They were to accomplish the miracle by the year 2020.

The third "goal" of the U.N.'s "Agenda 21" really pushed the envelope. It was an outlandish economic program that ordered the industrial nation's of the world to "cap" their pollution levels at a pre-determined figure. If they exceeded their caps, they would voluntarily transfer their wealth (send their money) to the non-polluting, still developing and very poor Third World Nations of the world.

In other words, they would "trade" money to exceed their pollution "caps" and the scam became known as "Cap and Trade". **The redistribution of wealth under a form of social-communism that Strong articulated five years previously at the Rio Earth Summit had now become a formal component of the U.N.'s "Agenda 21" document.**

A fourth goal of Agenda 21 is "Social Justice" which we will detail later.

Reflecting back to the 1970 Earth Day predictions of a coming "Ice Age" and the extermination of 80% of life on planet Earth had now been replaced by the new "Global Warming" threat to mankind. Unfortunately, few remembered those earlier years of history, just as Marcus Cicero warned.

Those nasty pop top cans that concerned us in the 1970s had long ago been "retooled" by beverage manufacturers, gone and largely forgotten. Our 1970 challenge to grocery shoppers ("save the trees, use plastic") was so far removed from the new United Nation's environmental reality; they could not possibly belong to the same movement, could they? In point of fact, they did not.

The Green Movement's evolution over 25 years had developed so slowly and incrementally, so deliberately and almost invisibly, that the 21st Century began with a planet that feared Global Warming and environmental extinction.

Like the Wizard of Oz who hid behind his curtain, pulled levers and made threatening noises that frightened the Cowardly Lion, the Tin Man, Dorothy and everybody in OZ, a small group of globalist wizards hiding behind a "Green Curtain" created one imagined environmental disaster after another. For two plus decades, the wizards scared everybody with their scientific eco-babble and demands for obedience to their Agenda for the 21st century. When they proclaimed "the science is settled", we were to have little doubt as to the severity of this threat.

The "Green Tsunami" began to build its strength around the planet with a giant and destructive wave of "green" rules and regulations, of do's and don'ts for the have's and have not's. In the mind of U.N. global environmentalists, the problems they manufactured in the 80s and 90s could only be solved by the U.N.'s Agenda for the new 21st century, an **"agenda" that was to continue until 2099.**

One might easily say, "This is just another conspiracy theory" since for many years "black helicopter" conspiracy theorists imagined a new world order was being secretly created at meetings of the Illuminati, or Freemasonry, or the Club of Rome. Perhaps, the Bilderbergers or the super-secret Tri Lateral Commission or even the New York City Council on Foreign Relations was at the heart of the global governance conspiracies.

In reality, the real proponents of "Globalism" operate completely in the open, supported by our tax dollars, in their New York City headquarters a tall, thin skyscraper along the East River. If the planet is to be safe from the threat of global warming and climate change, **the United Nations insists it knows what is best.** They have set their global agenda for the next century and it is moving incrementally forward. In fact, I would be willing to guess their work has already crept into your local community.

CHAPTER 3

THE U.N. — ASSORTED SCANDALS
AND CREEPY CHARACTERS

Since the 1945 creation of the U.N., the organization has now grown into a global behemoth. Sadly, most of us don't realize the size and scope of its global operations. There are six primary organizations, all functioning under the Secretary General's office in New York. Under those agencies there are another fifteen worldwide organizations that carry out the U.N.'s work and employ an army of roughly 40,000 workers.

The two most familiar operating bodies in the U.N. are the Security Council, where every member nation has the right of veto, and the General Assembly where the majority rules. Frankly, that majority of member nations are not America's friends and allies.

Largely, the U.N. is divided into two camps, the industrialized nations of the world and the developing, or Third World nations. The latter group sees the mission of the U.N. as "spreading the wealth around a little" seeking financial aid and development money from the more advanced industrial countries.

One of those advanced industrial countries is of course America. Of the U.N.'s General Operating budget, 25% of it is paid by only one of the U.N.'s 192 member nations—the United States. There are 135 members, who all get a vote in the General Assembly, but contribute a meager 1% to pay the U.N.'s bills. The annual budget for the United Nation's operation in NYC is $7 plus Billion.

Since its beginning, the U.N. has grown astronomically. At The Hague in the Netherlands sits the International Court of Justice, a full-blown U.N. operation. The fifteen justices who hear cases that involve international law are all elected by the General Assembly. I am willing to bet not one America can name any of the 15 faceless justices.

The court rules on such weighty controversies as crimes against humanity to matters involving genocide and war crimes. In the wrong hands, the U.N.'s International Court of Justice could decide that America's pursuit of a terrorist enemy with a drone attack anywhere in the world was a war crime and a U.S. government official could conceivably be put on trial. If an American drone strike caused civilian casualties, could the incident be labeled a genocide crime with military or government officials prosecuted at the U.N.'s International Court of Justice?

The World Court is but the first in a lengthy list of U.N. Agencies operating all over the world. Here is a fact worth noting. Although America pays a majority of the U.N.'s bills, few of the organizations operate within New York at the U.N. Headquarters, let alone anywhere inside our nation's borders.

For example, the U.N.'s Food and Drug Organization and U.N. Fund for Agricultural Development are both headquartered in Rome. The U.N.'s Civil Aviation Department is in Canada. UNESCO, the United Nations Education, Scientific and Cultural Organization, is headquartered within the shadow of Paris' Eiffel Tower. Offices for the U.N. Atomic Energy Commission and U.N. Office for Industrial Development are located in Vienna. Madrid, Spain is home to the U.N. office of International Tourism.

Geneva, Switzerland houses the U.N. office of the International Labor Organization, the U.N. International Telecommunications Union, the U.N. High Commission for Refugees and the U.N.'s World Health Organization that outlawed the use of D.D.T. back in the 1960s (a decision that has cost millions of lives, to this day, in developing nations).

Other Geneva offices include the World Intellectual Property Organization, the World Meteorological Association and the U.N. World Trade Organization. But before leaving Switzerland, we cannot forget the U.N.'s Postal Union in Berne. With so many U.N. offices already in Switzerland, is there any reason the entire U.N. operation should not be moved there? This would allow the Swiss to carry the financial burden.

The United States has managed to land only a handful of U.N. global operations. The largest monetary organization of the United Nations located in Washington, D.C. is the International Monetary Fund. This means if the U.N. has a money problem, the IMF is based near the center of America's monetary power. Then of course, there is the World Bank. Few realize that the World Bank is, in fact, a U.N. organization and under it three sub-operations; the International Bank for Reconstruction and Development, the International Finance Corporation and the International Center for the Settlement of Disputes. All are located in the sprawling and highly political inner-beltway of Washington, D.C. where U.S. currency printing operations are nearby.

The U.N. continues to maintain its standing army of "Peacekeepers". This global army currently has troops patrolling trouble spots in 117 countries. The U.N.'s peacekeepers are supported by more than 5,800 civilian staff members and the local civilian operations employ another 14,000. The annual budget for the U.N.'s standing army is more than $2 billion a year, again with America paying the largest percentage of the annual bill.

At any given year, the annual meeting of the General Assembly can create "special funds" which the U.N. bills to its members. **Therein lies a major problem that our government has complained about for decades—oversight. Essentially, there is none.** The U.N. operates with no public records and there is no U.N. Freedom of Information Act. Requests for operating information and budget details are routinely denied. Litanies of corruption scandals over the years, involving the U.N. and the Peacekeeper's army, have never been detailed.

During the George W. Bush presidency, America's dynamic U.N. Ambassador John Bolton broke the U.N. code of silence and released

447 documents containing thousands of pages of secret insider information. The revelations were startling:

- Bribes paid to local officials after the devastating tsunami in Indonesia.
- Sex crimes reported against U.N. Peacekeepers serving in the Gaza Strip.
- During the war in Kosovo, bribes were paid to a local U.N. official at the Kosovo Airport to get supplies to needy families.
- Reports of U.N. Peacekeepers stealing gold while patrolling The Congo.
- In Liberia, a U.N. Ukrainian pilot stole relief food and resold it.

American U.N. officials were also part of the scandals. Jacques Paul Klein, a U.S special representative to Liberia in Africa, quit his post in April of 2005. During the Bosnia War, his heavy-handed approach to his U.N. duties earned him the nickname "The Bully of Bosnia". President Bush had transferred Klein from Bosnia to Liberia where he struck up a relationship with a local woman who turned out to be a spy. An investigation into Klein showed he and his girlfriend used United Nation's aircraft as their private jets to attend U.N. parties and conferences all over the world.

The U.N. Oil for Food Program turned out to be another gigantic scandal. Designed to cripple the Saddam Hussein dictatorship in Iraq, an oil export embargo was imposed. But an exception was made to the crippling embargo, so Iraqi citizens were not harmed by the sanctions. Saddam was permitted to sell a small amount of the nation's crude to buy food and medicine for his people. The man who headed the U.N.'s Oil for Food program was the son of U.N. Secretary General Kofi Anan. To make a long and complex story as simple to understand as possible, the young businessman and his cronies became very wealthy men, Iraqi citizens suffered and Saddam laughed at both the U.N. and the U.S. Millions and perhaps billions of dollars were skimmed or diverted in complex financial schemes and no one was ever prosecuted.

Other U.N. Aid programs have been rife with corruption since the 1990s. The revolution in Cambodia required yet another U.N. Aid Program where administrators got rich and help did not trickle down to the local people. When the truth was eventually revealed, all of the U.N. officials mysteriously disappeared.

UNICEF, the United Nation's program known for their "Trick or Treat for UNICEF" Halloween fundraiser, was established in 1946 to feed the starving children, many of them orphans, left behind following WWII. The work of UNICEF evolved over the next five decades until the mission was expanded in the 1990s to include "advanced sexual and reproductive rights" taught to school children as young as 10 years of age. In 1987 in Belgium, a child porn ring operated out of the UNICEF headquarters involving pedophiles located in Switzerland, France and England. Fourteen were arrested in the sting. Shocking revelations at the trial proved that UNICEF do-gooders would ask for "sex relief" before they doled out aid to the needy kids. The UNICEF scandals were so abhorrent; that the U.S. Congress halted all financial support until UNICEF cleaned up their international act.

Compared to the long lists of scandals and corruption, the behavior of the U.N. staff in New York City is a relatively minor annoyance. Members are known throughout the city as "scofflaws". They notoriously drive cars with special U.N. diplomatic license plates, ignore parking and other minor traffic laws and when cited for violations simply never pay their tickets and claim diplomatic immunity.

At the New York Headquarters annual opening session of the General Assembly, news coverage reports a steady stream of global dictators who set up shop in nearby luxury hotels, tie up traffic as their motorcades drive them to the meeting and then parade to the marble podium to roundly condemn Israel and America. From the rambling and incoherent Iranian Mahmoud Ahmadinejad to Cuba's Fidel Castro and Venezuela's bellowing Hugo Chavez (both in healthier days); their speeches routinely receive long, standing ovations.

In light of the U.N.'s long history of scandals and corruption, one would think the world might have been more than a bit suspicious when a U.N. organization began issuing a steady stream of escalating global temperature readings claiming they were an imminent threat to the survival of all mankind. For years, we have been hearing that unless the world took drastic action to halt greenhouse gases, civilization would surely perish. And yet, somehow we are all still here.

The U.N. also engineered a global environmental program that would punish the rich and benefit the poor. Their reports determined the pollution caused by these developed nations created unimaginable harm to impoverished Third World countries, so "reparations" were in order. In other words, "Global Warming" was the reason for a giant redistribution of wealth as the U.N.'s Agenda 21 was implemented.

A small clique of elite U.N. scientists operating at the obscure East Anglia University in England became known as "The International Panel on Climate Change" but few realized it was top to bottom a U.N. organization. These "experts" became the world's leading source of global warming statistics for decades. Only a few "climate deniers" (or as I prefer to call them "environmental truth tellers") scrutinized the IPCC's alarming statistics. Most perplexing was how were these U.N. scientists able to construct temperature readings before the invention of the thermometer? The answer turned out to be uniquely revealing. They hired one "tree-ring" expert who charted the earth's temperatures from old logs he found dissected from around the world.

Then secret emails were revealed showing that from 2000 to 2006 one of the U.N.'s IPCC scientists at the East Anglia University School of Environmental Sciences and the director of the now-exposed Climate Research Unit received more than $19 million in U.N. research grants. That's approximately $3 million a year to "cook the climate books" and produce statistics that bolstered U.N. global warming claims.

Returning to our overview of U.N. operations around the world, the current available budget for all of the U.N.'s global operations in 2012 was introduced, voted on and passed Christmas Eve 2011 when most of the world's attention was otherwise occupied. Totaling a staggering $12.15 billion, it was divided between $5.15-billion for the General Budget and $7 billion for U.N. Peacekeeping Operations.

The U.S. was billed for 22% of the general budget and 27% of the U.N.'s standing army budget. In addition, we were billed for two of the U.N.'s special funds for the 2012 World Food Program and the U.N. Development Program.

Here is good news for Americans. After the revelation of the U.N.'s IPPC Climategate email scandal, Congress pulled the plug on the group's $13-million annual budget. Congress also told President Obama, his Environmental Protection Agency and EPA Secretary Lisa Jackson not to use any of their operating budgets to regulate greenhouse gases in America.

Now the bad news for Americans. The EPA and President Obama simply ignored the Congressional directive.

One final, cautionary thought about U.N. operations. They have a long history of proposing various "Global Tax" schemes, so they need no longer depend on the United States generosity to pay for their various U.N. global enterprises. The latest idea was a U.N. tax on all international transportation tickets, airfare and cruises. Alternately, they have suggested a tax on all overnight international monetary transfers within the global banking systems. If each transaction netted only a fraction of a penny, the globalists would receive an avalanche of income each night and would almost immediately be self supporting.

Imagine the U.N., an international globalist operation with an unlimited budget and no oversight. Imagine the mischief they could create. Knowing the socialist connections of Dr. Brundtland and the socialist/communist economic theories of Maurice Strong, how quickly might the U.N. move to impose a New One World Economy that would in turn support Global Governance and a New United Nations World Order? Could the radical environmentalists who are now suggesting a myriad of annoying behavior modifications, someday have a standing army to enforce their lifestyle changes and a world court to punish repeat offenders?

Remember, "Agenda 21" includes the three E's of sustainability—environment, economy and equity. Translated that means strict enforcement of environmental laws and regulations and a carefully regulated economy that is based on socialist-communist principals of equity redistribution as the U.N. takes from the rich and gives to the poor.

Come to think of it, that concept has already taken root in America.

CHAPTER 4

CREEPING GLOBALISM:
THE BRAVE, NEW, VERY GREEN WORLD

The desire to rule the world is as old as mankind.

From the Caesars of Rome to Alexander the Great, from Hitler's National Socialist Party to France's Napoleon Bonaparte and from Joseph Stalin's Union of Soviet Socialist Republics to the Islamic nations that terrorize the planet today, man has longed to impose his dominance on the other citizens of our planet. "Global Governance" is a modern day version of that age old desire. A small group of supposedly "enlightened elitists" will decide what is best for the rest of us.

Many are naturally suspicious of the planet being dominated by a one world government or a one world economic system. It simply sounds evil to those of us who love and cherish our freedoms. But globalism has made astounding gains in the past forty plus years. Since that first 1970 Earth Day, much of the U.N.'s progress has been under the benign banner of a supposedly well-intentioned, "green, environmental agenda".

After the first U.N. Earth Summit and follow-up "Agenda 21" meeting in Kyoto, Japan, The Brundtland Commission, Maurice

Strong, his wife Hanna and other U.N. officials were preparing to shift their global environmental agenda into overdrive. But they had one fundamental problem; few in America trust the United Nations.

In the 1970s, virtually every bus bench at public transit stops in California was used by the John Birch Society to advertise their plea, "Get US out of the United Nations". And yet for years and unexplained reasons, America has simply agreed to foot the bill for an organization, with an international cadre of fellow international travelers, who take delight in giving standing ovations to two-bit dictators and assorted despots from around the world while seeminly enjoying their opposition to America's vision of freedom and democracy.

The U.N. was also very aware of their tarnished reputation that resulted from that ever growing list of international scandals. As they unrolled "Agenda 21" with all of its socialist/communist philosophy, they studiously avoided being an overt presence in the climate hysteria of the 1980s and 90s. But the globalists were nonetheless working furiously behind their "green curtain", pulling the levers and making lots of threatening noises to cause climate panic around the world.

The U.N.'s claims of Acid Rain or a Hole in the Ozone layer were boosted by the scientific information spoon-fed to the world for two decades by that shadowy group of scholars gathered under the relatively innocuous name, "The International Panel on Climate Change" —the IPCC. They were clever enough not to call the panel a U.N. study group, thereby avoiding the general mistrust of the U.N.'s branding and instead referring to it as an "international" panel.

"Climate Change" eventually replaced and updated the more general threat of "Global Warming" as put forth in Agenda 21 because, quite honestly, the planet was not cooperating. For 16 of the last 18 years, scientists tell us the earth simply has not warmed. In fact, they tell us that more recently, global temperatures have started to fall. Conversely, this meant the newest environmental threat was actually as old as the first Earth Day. Was our planet heading for a "Global Cooling" period that the Ice Agers predicted lo, those many years ago?

Yet not to be dissuaded from the necessity for the Global Warming debate, global environmentalists recently released temperature readings claiming America's temperatures in 2012 were the warmest in history, certain proof that global warming was indeed happening. And to add even more evidence to their argument, in late October of 2012, two weather fronts combined to create an unprecedented storm called "Hurricane Sandy". There indeed was the obvious proof—dangerous storms increasing, ocean levels rising, and no doubt, "the sky was falling". Once again the environmental hand wringers roared on national television, "Beware, we are destroying the planet and we must take action now!"

However, to repudiate those claims, scientists—bona fide ones—were quick to remind us, if the U.S. had an unusually warm spate of weather for one or two years, it doesn't mean the rest of the planet is overheating. Our country actually makes up about 1.6% of the total earth's surface. In fact, climate records actually show the hottest days ever recorded in American history was in the1930s at the start of the Industrial Revolution, before there was smog and little air pollution. Then, New York City temperatures were over one hundred degrees for weeks at a time and in the southwestern United States, the Dust Bowl occurred because of the record heat and drought. Nothing quite as catastrophic has happened in America since.

I received an interesting chart and email from Dr. Roy Spencer, who has for many years approached the environmental dooms-day prophets with a mostly skeptical eye. In early 2013, while the television newscasters were touting the preceding year as the hottest year on record...ever, he wrote, "Since 1979, NOAA satellites have been carrying instruments which measure the natural microwave thermal emissions from oxygen in the atmosphere," says his note. "John Christy and I update global temperature datasets that represent the piecing together of the temperature data from a total of eleven instruments flying on eleven different satellites over the years." He updates his charts the first week of every month and publishes them for everyone to see at his website listed in the back of this book.

Here is his graph. It traces the temperatures across the planet since America launched the first of our NOAA satellites in the late 70s'. As you read the graph, note: an El Nino event occurred in 1997-98 when the earth's temperatures literally skyrocketed. But by 2008, the graph returns to normal and stays closer to the center until 2011 when it shows another drop, thus the concept that we may be entering a period of global cooling.

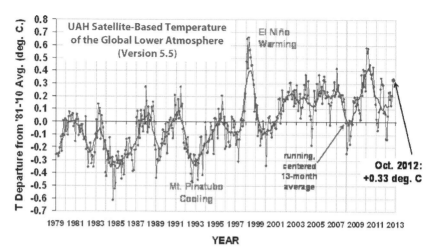

Roy Spencer graph

To give you a comparison, the U.N.'s IPCC scientists have, for many years, produced their own charts and graphs to prove the theory of "Global Warming". Their purpose is not to relay scientific findings, as we shall soon demonstrate. The goal of the Intergovernmental Panel on Climate Change, sponsored by the U.N., was to produce materials that bolstered the U.N. Agenda 21 environmental claims. The most well-known of their graphs is the "hockey stick graph" made popular by Al Gore in his film "An Inconvenient Truth".

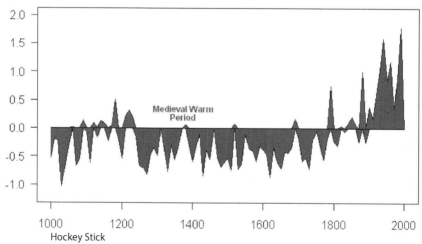

Hockey Stick

Dr. Spencer's graph depicts temperatures recorded by satellites since the orbiters were launched in 1979. The second graph reconstructs the Earth's Temperatures back to a time when man's knowledge of astro-physics was, shall we say, somewhat more crude than it is today.

We have learned a great deal about the inner workings of the U.N.'s IPCC climate scientists who work at an obscure English East Anglia University. For years, the IPCC scientific work was shrouded in mystery and many marveled that this small group of scientists with glowing credentials and the stamp of approval from the U.N. constantly seemed to contradict the research of men like Roy Spencer and thousands of other scientists. How could the IPCC prove, beyond any shadow of a doubt, there is a fragile canopy of atmosphere surrounding our earth that it is trapping gases, which they named "The Greenhouse Effect", and that those gases are warming our planet at a lethal and increasingly rapid pace? As we now know, the scientists were "cooking the books".

In 2009, computer hackers (whose identity remains to this day a very well guarded secret) entered the dark recesses of the scientist's email accounts and revealed a global environmental scandal that became known as "Climategate". Over 1,000 of their secret communications were made public in Phase One and a few years later, a second release of documents was made public. Page upon page revealed how British and American scientists were manipulating data. As they programmed their computers to predict the earth's impending climate change catastrophe on the "hockey stick graph" and others, they included statistics that proved their hypothesis while conveniently omitting the rest of the data.

Garbage in, garbage out.

We also learned that millions of dollars of "research grants" were awarded to the various IPCC scientists over the years with but one stipulation; **their work must prove the "Global Warming" theory with science that was irrefutable.** If anyone dare to come snooping around under something called the U.S. Freedom of Information Act, they were told, "Simply ignore them. You work for the U.N. and we don't have any stinkin' Freedom of Information Act."

Governments around the globe, including our own, unquestioningly believed everything the IPCC team published. Anyone who challenged their data was ridiculed by a compliant global media. In turn, national governments poured billions, perhaps trillions of dollars into the phony science that eventually trickled down the bureaucratic food chain as local and state governments based their planning models on the flawed East Anglia University research.

Now, two decades after the theory of global warming was first floated in 1992 at the Rio Earth Summit, the global agenda to impose The Brundtland Commission's "Our Common Future", Hannah Strong's "Earth Charter" and her hubby's call for a socialist/communist economic new world order, a "Green Tsunami" of alternative energy solutions and strategic "sustainable" planning are being packaged for local consumption under the name "The International Council for Local Environmental Initiatives" (ICLEI), pronounced "Ick'- lee". We will discuss ICLEI and many of their shrouded U.N. "Agenda 21" environmental programs in the following chapter.

Once again, the U.N. has strategically chosen not to identify ICLEI, much like the IPCC, calling it an "International" group. But with a few clicks of your computer's mouse you can easily access the ICLEI website on the internet and learn that the international movement is yet again, another aggressive U.N. organization. They are using their immense global power and lots of international money to implement "Agenda 21" in local communities throughout the world creating more basic building blocks for their vision of a One World Government. As we continue collecting the dots, the "Green Tsunami" gains energy.

CHAPTER 5

ICLEI: THE BIG BAD WOLF
HUFFING AND PUFFING AT YOUR DOOR

How could the nations of the world be convinced to forsake their independence and sovereignty and voluntarily join a One World Government or a New World Order?

Throughout man's history, dictators have used force, both in military and economics, to grind those who are weaker into surrendering their national allegiance and joining a march toward world domination. But short of a military invasion, or the threat of one, would any sovereign government simply relinquish its independence and sovereignty?

That problem has been solved by a new globalist concept known as "regionalism". For a variety of reasons, nations of the world might be convinced to join regional alliances because once they do; regions can easily be linked together. Twentieth century Europe is an excellent example.

After the fall of the Berlin Wall and the "perestroika" of the Soviet Union, two regionalism concepts were introduced in Europe; militarily, the NATO alliance and economically, the European Common Market or the European Union (EU).

Since the birth of the EU, all local monetary currencies—the pound, the lira, the punt—have been folded into the newly minted Euro. Passports and visas are no longer needed to travel between Britain and Turkey. Trade restrictions, labor laws, tariffs and other economic factors have been folded into the fabric of the EU, while NATO forms the military umbrella. But all has not gone as planned in the EU. In fact, England and Germany, with decades of experience keeping less dependable partners in other nations afloat, is now considering withdrawing.

Nonetheless, regionalism accelerated toward the end of the 20th century. The North American Free Trade Association linked Canada, Mexico and the United States. In Tokyo, there is a similar Pan-Asian Trading Community. The world is gradually moving toward regionalism and the global governance promoters still believe that regional governments can more easily and seamlessly be blended into a New World Order, bypassing national sovereignty.

Consider how many times America has refused to move unilaterally when confronted with a military challenge. Before taking defensive or offensive action, the government has consulted with "the international community" or "our partners" to form mostly imaginary coalition forces that respond to threats.

A French businessman who served as the director of the European Commission for Trade, Director-General Pascal Lamy, currently heads the U.N.'s World Trade Organization. In a speech at Oxford University on March 8, 2012, Mr. Lamy summed up the current view of regionalism leading to globalism by stating, "In the absence of truly global government, global governance results from the action of several states. It is inter-national, between nations. In other words, global governance is the globalization of local governance."

The Director-General further explained new Regionalism leads directly to a "one world government" based on a "one world economy", and described his theory as a three sided triangle:

Side One of the Triangle

Trade groups like the G-20 replaced the outdated G-8. As new members joined the group, G-20's economic influence has expanded to include more partners aligned with common goals and actions—a microcosm of regionalism.

Side Two of the Triangle

The United Nations. This global body will lead and direct the voluntary cooperation among regional groups for mutual aid and assistance, resulting in UN global governance.

Side Three of The Lamy Triangle

"Member-driven International Organizations". Non-governmental agencies (NGO's) will meet to solve local and regional problems and provide specialized rules, policies and/or programs that will provide regional solutions. The step from regionalism to globalism is viewed by Lamy and others as merely a small baby step to a "New World Order".

Pascal Lamy
G-20 and the Path to Global Governance

Pascal Lamy Triangle

What Lamy described was a U.N. project launched in New York in 1990, one that has been steadily growing for 20 plus years. The Organization's motto is, "think globally and act locally". This relatively unpublicized agency specifically targets the cooperative interrelationship of local governments all over the earth. By the thousands, cities and counties, most times unwittingly, have signed on to the new U.N. agency, voluntarily paid their dues to join and are now actively implementing Agenda 21's global goals into local government. Here is how it happened.

Two years before the 1992 Rio Earth Summit convened with Strong and Brundtland's synchronized socialist influence, the International Council for Local Environmental Initiatives, known as ICLEI was created by the United Nations. Alternately, it is known as "The World Congress of Local Governments for a Sustainable Future" and by now, your local city or county government might well be a "Gold Star" member.

In its first two decades, ICLEI has been able to establish 14 global offices. They now have members in 70 different nations with more than 1,220 local governments signed on as members. ICLEI claims their member organizations around the world represent a total of 569,885,000 people with a substantial portion of the world's population pledging through their local governments, to support the goals of the U.N.'s Agenda 21.

At the ICLEI website, their goal is laid out quite clearly: "ICLEI supports local governments in finding and implementing local solutions to global challenges". They go on to to explain, "Our programs and projects advocate participatory, long-term strategic planning processes that address local sustainability (there's that key code word again) while protecting global common goods. This approach links local action and solutions to the global challenges we are facing and therefore also links local action to global goals and targets."

Such a grand, global scheme requires both money and international prestige to accomplish its goals. The sponsors of ICLEI offer the U.N. both influence and money. Among the U.N.'s ICLEI sponsors are United Cities and Local Governments, The World Economic Forum, The World Bank, The Clinton Climate Initiative, the World Conservation Union, and many other major and well-known global environmental groups. **NOTE: (Bill and Hillary's charity meet annually in New York City the week prior to the opening of the U.N. General Assembly. Attendance is by invitation only and closed to the media.)**

Naively, many believe these well-known environmental organizations are simply a collection of well meaning bird watchers wearing funny hats, sensible shoes and taking pictures of exotic species while strolling through local parks and wetlands. Nothing could be further from the truth. In fact, here are some of the members from President Clinton's "Council On Sustainable Development" mentioned in Chapter 2.

The granddaddy of environmental groups is the Sierra Club, headquartered in San Francisco and founded in 1892 by John Muir, iconic naturalist and Yosemite Valley hiker. But in 1969, a schism within the group forced long time member David Browner to be removed from the Sierra Club board for being too controversial. He immediately formed his own environmental organization, Friends of the Earth. Less one think Friends of the Earth is a laid back group of bird watchers, their website affirms they are "an environmental non-governmental organization (NGO) with observer status at several intergovernmental organizations (such as FAO, IMO, UNEP), and the International Whaling Commission." They state their objectives quite clearly, "to protect the Earth against deterioration and to repair damage inflicted upon the environment as a result of human activity and negligence; to preserve the Earth's ecological, cultural, and ethnic diversity; to increase public participation and democratic decision making in the protection of the environment and the management of natural resources; to achieve social, economic, and political justice and equal access to resources and opportunities on a local, national, and international level; and to promote environmental sustainable development on a local, national, and global level."

Friends of the Earth proudly take credit for the media campaign that successfully halted construction of the Canadian XL Pipeline in the United States. The group is supported by an incredible 4,034,240 members worldwide.

Another well-known environmental activist group, Greenpeace, dates back to the early 1970s evolving from the anti-war movement and anti-nuclear protests. Today, they are also a non-governmental (environmental) organization, another "NGO", with a goal to "ensure the ability of the Earth to nurture life in all its diversity and focuses its campaigning on world wide issues such as global warming, deforestation, overfishing, commercial whaling, genetic engineering and anti-nuclear issues." They claim to raise money from "2.9 million individual supporters and foundation grants".

But the environmental group considered by many to be the most powerful in the world is the Natural Resources Defense Council (NRDC) headquartered in New York City. It is a coalition of 300 environmental attorneys backed by a few *carefully selected scientists* who provide data for the group's lawsuits.

NRDC spokespersons appear routinely in the mainstream media and are frequently quoted as expert environmentalists. But it is their team of activist attorneys who file environmental lawsuits with the courts nationally, regionally and locally. Next time you hear of an environmental legal action, chances are the mega-lawyer firm, the Natural Resources Defense Council, is involved.

Another huge international, environmental group is The Nature Conservancy. As of 2009, they boast of assets of $5.64-billion. Leading the Nature Conservancy is President and CEO Mark Tercek who was once a managing director at Goldman Sachs. With over one million due paying members in 30 countries, the organization claims it has protected 119 million acres of land throughout the world and 5,000 miles of rivers and streams since it began operations in 1951.

Dozens of non-governmental organizations (NGO's) bring their environmental agenda and substantial financial support to fund the work of ICLEI. Their websites make no secret of how they raise money by declaring "We have a wide range of international partners that collaborate on our programs and campaigns, including national governments, academic institutions, local project-specific partners such as foundations and non-governmental organizations, and dozens of national, regional and international associations of local governments."

ICLEI is another U.N. organization headquartered outside of the United States in Bonn, Germany. With offices in 12 major cities dotted strategically around the globe, ICLEI directs their work through regional offices in Oakland, California; Capetown, South Africa; Toronto, Canada and Tokyo. The European Secretariat is located in Freiburg, Germany and the Latin American and Caribbean Secretariat is in Sao Paulo Brazil. There are other offices in Mexico, Melbourne, Australia; New Delhi, India; and Manila, The Philippines.

On January 1, 2013, Gino Van Begin took control of the international ICLEI operations. Since 2000, he served as the regional director of operations at the ICLEI European Secretariat. Before that appointment, he served as the head of the EU's Environmental Centers in Russia, at Kaliningrad and St. Petersburg. Born in Belgium, Van Begin co-drafted a document known as "The Aalborg Commitments on Urban Sustainability", a regional planning program that currently includes 600 cities and towns.

Van Begin was preceded at ICLEI by the former World Secretariat, Konrad Otto Zimmerman, who was installed as the first ICLEI Chairman when the U.N. group was launched in 1992. A lifetime environmentalist and like Van Begin an urban planner, he is a member of the United Nation's Program for Environmental Governance and the World Economic Forum's Global Agenda Council.

Every three years, ICLEI stages a large World Conference and according to their website connects "experts and peers from around the globe to share challenges and learn the most successful strategies for local sustainability and forge common solutions".

Tactically, in America ICLEI implements their globalist environmental agenda through regional planning groups. Many of them bypass locally elected officials. City and County planners subscribe to ICLEI's guidelines and when, for example, they apply for state and federal funding for regionally-planned projects, ICLEI membership virtually assures funding.

ICLEI's United States President and Board Chairman is a not-so-well-known and remarkably unlikely U.S. mayor, by the name of Patrick Hays, from the city of North Little Rock, Arkansas. He is assisted by the ICLEI-U.S.A. Corporate Secretary, Pegeen Hanrahan, former Mayor of Gainesville, Florida and ICLEI-U.S.A. Corporate Treasurer, Frank Cownie, former mayor of Des Moines, Iowa.

Are all of these small town politicians and regional urban planners a network of Global Environmental Conspirators bent on undermining U.S. sovereignty and creating a New World Order? Of course not. But, like many government officials all over the world, they became convinced during the 1990s that the goals of "Agenda 21" and the United Nations could solve the international environmental crisis of "Global Warming".

ICLEI is very active across America. While they might seem relatively benign at first glance with a global environmental agenda as their goal, here are a few of the more enticing ICLEI news story headlines listed on their website.

- "EPA Releases Document on Energy Efficiency in Local Government Operations"
- "City of Houston joins Better Buildings Challenge"

- "Carpentaria, CA Switches to LED Street Lighting to Cut Costs"
- "Seattle's Green Building Evolution"
- "Earth Day Network announces cities that will participate in Clinton Global Initiative"
- "Ithaca, NY goes 100% renewable"
- "Learn more about your state and local GHG emissions with EPA's new map tool!"

Remember, most of the ICLEI goals and strategies are being implemented, not at the federal or state level, but by regional planning boards bypassing local voter accountability.

Consider the story of the city of Danville, California where this town's general plan was put together by an unelected Regional Planning Commission. As introduced, the proposal will guide the city's development for the next 20 years. Danville has joined a regional group known as the "Association of Bay Area Governments" and the group's bonding commitment is the implementation of the U.N.'s "Agenda 21".

One Danville resident who studied the regional plan observed it is full of "eco-babble", the same eco-babble that has become familiar to all of us through the mainstream media. The planners address the usual list of environmental issues like "sustainable action, environmental preservation and reducing greenhouse gases". The regional planners, determined that downtown Danville will become "a priority development area", designed a network of transportation corridors that will enable the city to compete for federal, state and local funds for road maintenance and improvements. In the downtown area, the city also plans to set aside more than nine acres of prime real estate for new high density and affordable housing located adjacent to public transportation stops. This is an "Agenda 21" concept known as "pack and stack"—high rise apartment living. Global environmentalists believe it will be the future of urban housing.

Like Danville, cities across America are adopting the same concept. Regional planners are creating networks of transportation corridors that embrace the U.N.'s "Agenda 21" sustainability goals, including public transportation systems that will have not-too-frequent stops at stations where low income, high rise housing (environmentally engineered apartments) will be located. ICLEI's goal for the current century is to popularize communities where cooperative "global citizens" won't demand private transportation and certainly won't demand an energy gobbling, 2300 square foot private home. Instead, they will live happily in an 800 square foot apartment, stacked one atop the other. The green citizens of the future will happily walk to the nearest public transportation stop where they can catch a ride to work or to shop. Better yet, they can bike to their destination on new taxpayer-supported bike paths. A "Green Utopia" will have finally come to our planet.

With three quick steps on the internet, you can read about ICLEI for yourself:

- First: Enter ICLEI.org in your browser to get their website.
- Second: Look for the tab labeled "Programs" and click on it.
- Third: Scroll down until you find Agenda 21 and voila!

From sea to shining sea, citizens in western cities from Spokane, Washington and Santa Rosa, California to east coast cities in states like Maryland, Pennsylvania and Virginia, residents are getting informed about the globalist intentions of the U.N.'s ICLEI program. They are learning how these plans are being subversively implemented, bypassing their locally-elected officials.

ICLEI's "Think globally—Act locally" slogan doesn't make sense to most Americans. Our nation's long history of individual freedom and representative democracy is at odds with the ICLEI concept of elitist government policy from the top down. And in America's current economic climate, tax dollars are in short supply. When local citizens learn their local government is sending membership dues to ICLEI, either through the U.N. headquarters in New York or the ICLEI headquarters in Germany, citizens are outraged and demand it be stopped.

As regional planners realized they were under attack, their national umbrella organization, The American Planning Association (APA), issued a list of "talking points" explaining their work in glowing terminology in an effort to help local planners defend themselves from outraged citizens. "APA members help create communities of lasting value," the directive begins. "Good planning helps create communities that offer better choices for where and how people work and live. And planning enables civic leaders, business interests and citizens to play a meaningful role in creating communities that enrich people's lives."

The APA's "Glossary for the Public" document goes on to say that "some opponents of planning argue... that sustainable development... adversely affects not only an individual's rights and freedoms but also true local control. Given such a perspective, it is imperative that planners frame discussions about sustainability, regionalism, livability and the like (see trigger words below) in a way that emphasizes the economic value, long-lasting benefits and positive outcomes that result from good planning and plan implementation."

APA's CEO Paul Farmer, who obviously understands the coming wave of public criticism has sent his talking points memo to hundreds of regional planners to arm them in public debate. "As planning and planners have become targets of suspicion and mistrust, it is more important than ever to avoid polarizing jargon, to focus on outcomes important to local citizens and to maintain a fair, open and transparent process," Farmer's talking points document states.

Still, citizens who have investigated these regional planning groups and their embrace of the ICLEI goals of "Agenda 21"and sustainability read Farmer's words and strongly disagree. To the average citizen who learns his tax dollars intended for road repair and construction of freeways, are being diverted to pay for ICLEI membership and a U.N. environmental/globalism agenda, see nothing fair, open or transparent in any of the APA's eco-babble.

CHAPTER 6

AL GORE'S ROAD SHOW:
AN ENVIROMENTAL SNOW JOB

Before we connect the dots between globalism, regionalism, the United Nations, Agenda 21 and ICLEI, any comprehensive review of sustainable development's growth the last 15 years would be found lacking if it did not include the "environmental skullduggery" of Al Gore. As reported earlier, his 1990's book "Earth in the Balance" became a game changer in the campaign to popularize the pseudo-science of "Global Warming" and "Climate Change".

Historically, when Al was defeated in the 2000 Presidential election by a few "hanging chads", many believed he was cheated out of the presidency. With a giant block of public sentiment behind him, Al got a boost with his soon to be post-presidential careers as an environmental venture capitalist and a preacher of his "Global Warming" gospel. Al was a natural draw for earnest young college students who, by nature, mistrusted government institutions. A candidate swindled out of the presidency was someone they welcomed and earnestly listened to.

In 2004 while speaking on the UCLA campus in Southern California, Al drew the attention of an environmental activist in the audience, Laurie David. She was the wife of Larry David, renowned television producer of the shows "Seinfeld" and "Curb Your Enthusiasm". Mrs. David suggested for Al's talk to reach a much larger audience it needed to become a major motion picture. With Laurie David as a member of the Board of Trustees for the aforementioned Natural Resources Defense Council, Al's subject matter fit perfectly with Mrs. David's and the NRDC's agenda. Laurie's use of her considerable connections in both Hollywood and New York and all the glitz and star power she could muster contributed to Al's power point presentation becoming the movie, "An Inconvenient Truth". An Oscar and Nobel Peace Prize followed and Al and "Global Warming" had hit the street running.

Candidly, behind every gleaming moment of Al Gore's successes, there has always been a shadow of misfortune. Since his early days in politics to his most recent network television enterprise, miscalculation and mischief seem to follow him wherever he goes.

During his presidential campaign, one such bizarre incident involved a typical luncheon fund raiser at a Buddhist Temple in Hacienda Heights, CA, a small community just east of downtown Los Angeles. Among other guests, Al's audience included the saffron-robed monks who take an obligatory vow of poverty as they become priests in their religious order. Yet somehow, Gore's presidential campaign managed to collect contributions at the luncheon of more than $100,000.

An investigation soon followed. The monks were called before a Congressional Investigating Committee asking them who arranged the function and most important who donated all that money? As a result of the investigation, twenty co-conspirators (fortunately none of them Buddhist monks) went to jail for their part in the fiasco. Many suspected a sinister plot by the Chinese government to exert influence on America's presidential election was somehow behind the scam. Al publicly mumbled something about "no controlling legal authority" and the mainstream media and the U.S. Congress gave Al and his presidential campaign a free pass.

Even Al's Nobel Peace Prize was tainted, as he shared it with the now-disgraced U.N. organization, the International Panel on Climate Change (the IPCC). You remember them, the U.N. scientists who cooked the "climate books" all those years in favor of "Global Warming".

In England, Al's film was shown in public school classrooms. English parents, skeptical of the outrageous claims Gore made in his film, demanded the schools stop showing his movie. When that failed, the parents filed a formal lawsuit with the London High Court and demanded Gore prove his environmental claims or admit they were false. Evidence from both sides was weighed at trial and the esteemed judge ruled, "The Armageddon scenario that he depicts.... is not based on any scientific view."

The judge ordered whenever Al's movie was shown to English school children, each impressionable child must be given a 77-page booklet detailing the nine specific central errors contained in "An Inconvenient Truth". As Republican political analyst, Karl Rove, says with a chuckle, "Al doesn't tell Whoppers, he tells double-patty with cheese, super-sized Whoppers." However, do you recall reading about the trial in any national or local newspapers? .

"An Inconvenient Truth" has turned out to be, at the very least, "An Inconsistent Truth". The public was sold a marvelous fictional account of impending disaster that rivals anything published since the fables of C.S Lewis, H. R. R. Tolkien and Harry Potter combined. Governments have accepted the eco-babble as fact and spent billions, if not trillions, of dollars to perpetuate environmental myths.

As we revisit Al's fantastic claims, more and more of them are being revealed as the hoax they truly are. First and foremost, the globe is not warming. In fact, as previously referenced, in 16 of the last 18 years the Earth's temperature has remained more or less unchanged. Recently it has, almost unbelievably, started to cool. That cooling trend is now the major concern of virtually every climate scientist around the earth, the exact opposite of Al's global warming scenario.

Second, remember Al's claim that the Himalayan glaciers were melting and would disappear by the year 2035? Turns out that story was printed in 1999 in "New Science" magazine and was an off handed quote attributed to a pair of environmental hikers, not scientists, not scientific observers, but two hikers. The story appeared in print and fit neatly into Al's "Global Warming" scenario, so he included it in his movie. For years, it was considered an indisputable fact. Now, the Himalayan glacier myth has melted but the glaciers are still there, as icy and cold as ever. "New Science" magazine has since retracted the story, but not Al or the mainstream media.

No doubt, we all remember those hopeless white polar bears in Al's movie seen floating on a small chunk of ice. While there is good news for polar bear fans, there is bad news for the environmental alarmists. According to the America's Fish and Wildlife Service latest polar bear census, the polar bears are multiplying abundantly. As a matter of fact, the natives who live in the Arctic wilds are asking the bears be removed from the "Endangered Species" list so they can be hunted, lest they over-populate the area and threaten the local citizenry.

One of the grandest claims made in Al's film was rising ocean levels causing another ocean crisis. Because the glaciers and ice fields were melting, coastal cities around the world would be flooded within the predictable future. Las Vegas would become a beach front community and perhaps Pittsburg, PA as well. Rising oceans would surely inundate the populated islands in the South Pacific and the Caribbean. Flooding of the islands would forever change civilization as we know it. All, of course, are foolish predictions that simply haven't happened the way Al told us they would.

The oceans of the world are very accurately measured by ocean buoys that are strategically placed all over the planet. A colleague of mine, Lord Christopher Monkton (who served as Margaret Thatcher's environmental advisor), sent me an email reporting that the oceans of the world "will rise about 1 inch (you read that right, one inch) during the next century" (yes, a one inch rise in the next 100 years). Lord Monckton is nothing short of a genius and his website is an encyclopedia of common sense environmentalism that doesn't mince words. You will find it listed in the back of this book.

As Gore raked in massive profits from his film career and received global accolades for his courageous reporting about the earth's impending environmental disasters, he began rethinking his career as an environmental advocate. He decided to purse a second career path, that of an "environmental investor". In 2006, Gore was invited to join as full partner in the Silicon Valley venture capitol firm, Kleiner Perkins Caulfield & Byers (KPCB), who provided funding for a great deal of Silicon Valley's pioneers. Many predicted Al would soon become the world's first "Carbon Billionaire".

Gore's investments in an astounding array of environmental projects have indeed added to his incredible wealth. Unfortunately, that cloud of misfortune has followed Al into this newest career being known now as a "do as I say, not as I do" environmentalist.

Al owns four homes across the country. One is located in Arlington, Virginia across the Potomac River from the nation's capitol and another located in Carthage, Tennessee in the district he represented as a U.S. Senator. He purchased a third home in Nashville with an expansive 20 rooms and 10,000 square feet of living space. But it has become nothing short of an environmental public relations disaster. The mansion reportedly uses more than 30 times the annual electricity than the average Nashville electric customer with not a single solar panel in sight.

A few years ago, Al bought his fourth home, best described as a mega-estate in Montecito, California. The asking price for the mansion was $8.8 million dollars. Not bad for a former presidential candidate who was hustling college speaking dates after his loss in the 2000 election. Pictures of the new Gore "California Palace" can be found online with not one visible solar panel anywhere.

To say that Al's fortunes have increased significantly in recent years would be something of a gross understatement. However, during an August 2011 speech he delivered at The Aspen Institute in Colorado, the first visible chinks in Al's always-confident demeanor were exposed.

Al began his talk slowly and somewhat defensively claiming that "special interest groups were paying pseudo-scientists to pretend to be scientists and put out the message, 'this climate thing, it's nonsense'. Manmade CO-2 doesn't trap heat," he said. And then he shocked the audience as he shouted into the microphone, "Bull-****!"

He continued his tirade, "It may be sunspots. Bull****!"

It's not getting warmer. Bull****!"

"It's no longer acceptable in mixed company, meaning bipartisan company, to use the G**-damn word 'climate'".

The man who once claimed he invented the internet soon found his unfortunate meltdown had gone viral.

As the year 2012 came to a close, Gore was finalizing the sale of his failing television network, Current TV, to a company backed by the oil-rich, Middle East nation of Qatar, a country that has become sickeningly wealthy by selling Al's dreaded "fossil fuels" to the rest of the world. Remember, in his movie "An Inconvenient Truth", he claimed fossil fuels were the cause of CO-2 emissions and they in turn caused global warming. Al, as an investor, not an advocate, is a 20% owner of the Current TV network. His take of the $500,000,000 deal netted Al a tidy check for $100 million.

Glen Beck revealed publically that his communications company, Mercury, offered to buy Current TV from Gore. Apparently, Beck's conservative viewpoint didn't fit Gore's agenda. According to a press release from Gore, following the transaction, Al Jazeera television seemed a better fit. By the way, this is the network in the Middle East that once posted beheadings by Al Qaeda terrorists, but yet seemed more aligned with Gore's philosophy of hard hitting television news reporting.

The transaction has fallen under a tad bit of scrutiny from the mainstream media. In a recent interview on NBC's "Today Show", Matt Lauer suggested Al was guilty of hypocrisy. Al said he understood the view point but disagreed with the reasoning.

Al is a wealthy man, but must be unhappy with his film completely discredited, full of factual errors and his Nobel Peace Prize shared with a bunch of U.N. sponsored scientists who have been found wanting. The mainstream media continues to beat his "environmental drum" as though nothing has happened while our local, state, federal and international governments continue to use his fanciful conclusions as the basis for economic policy and massive investments of scarce public tax dollars.

His phony globalist environmental agenda continues to be foisted on our local communities in the name of the United Nation's "Agenda 21" ICLEI programs. However, as American citizens are getting informed they are beginning to push back.

Recalling the John Birch Society '70s slogan, "Get the U.S. out of the U.N." coupled with decades of Americans demanding "Get the U.N. out of America", now more than ever both have become a renewed rallying cry across the nation.

CHAPTER 7

GREEN BACKS INVESTED
IN GREEN ENERGY DISASTERS

Consider how far the goals of global environmentalists have crept into our federal government and the astounding number of green-energy businesses that have been given federal loans from the U.S. Department of Energy and then quickly went bankrupt.

Solyndra is probably the best known example of green investment gone awry, though the business was only awarded a $535-million loan guarantee. To date, 36 firms that received federal assistance for their "green energy" projects have either gone bust, are preparing to enter bankruptcy or have begun *laying* off workers instead of *growing* green jobs.

Sunpower was a solar project that received $1.2 billion, First Solar received $1.46 billion and Brightsource Energy pulled in $1.6 billion—all from Uncle Stupid in D.C. Not including those three green investments, thirty three other projects received over $2,812,000,000 of wasted federal tax money. If President Obama's second inaugural address is any indication, plans for dozens of "investments" into green projects are on the federal fast track before he leaves office in 2016.

Tax dollars have also supported electric car companies. The Tesla and Fisker electric car manufacturers have yet to become household names. Why? Because both have spent their federal money to create pricey, battery driven vehicles that buyers simply aren't buying. Fisker alone received $529-million to mass produce an affordable all-electric car. Now they too have gone under, still owing $200 million to the American taxpayers, while two Chinese companies are in a bidding war to purchase them.

Speaking of Chinese companies, another one has swooped in and purchased the bankrupt American battery company A123 for a cool $260 million. A mere $249 million was awarded A123 in 2009 from the stimulus/taxpayers "green energy pot".

General Motors (GM), now known affectionately as "Government Motors", received federal bailout money and put their pricey, all electric Volt on the market. Although they have tried every imaginable marketing ploy, they have been spectacularly unsuccessful at creating buyers. Production has now been halted.

Millions more of our tax money has been invested in the construction of electric car-charging stations for the non-existent fleet of all electric cars. Tennessee is a perfect example of lots of charging stations with a handful of electric cars to service. In some states, gas station owners have been ordered by local, regional, state and federal officials to install electric car charging stations right next to their gas pumps.

Also, billions of tax dollars have been used to construct industrial strength windmill farms and mega-solar plants. Promises at ribbon cutting ceremonies always sound great but delivering on them has been a long and difficult process. Those nasty unintended consequences that government has become so famous in assuring never disappoint with one problem, delay or closure after another.

In California, along a major desert highway leading to the state's border with Nevada, several astoundingly large solar projects are under construction. Three are being built in America's largest county, San Bernardino, where they cover an astounding 22,000 acres of desert land. That translates into 43 square miles.

The Ivanpah Solar Project is one of the three and includes a total of 170,000 garage-door-size solar mirrors. Each is automatically adjusted every ten seconds by a GPS system that tracks the sun. The mirrors reflect sunlight into three, 45-story water storage towers where the water is heated to 1,000 degrees. That hot water creates steam power that generates the electricity. When completed, the project will be the largest solar plant of its kind anywhere in the world. That claim is easily justifiable for one simple reason; no one has ever tried this complicated form of solar power generation before, anywhere.

Will it work? That's anybody's guess. But that much feared "law of unintended consequences" has already raised its ugly head in the Ivanpah construction project. For 220 million years, the desert has been home to the Desert Tortoise. No surprise, it is a species found on the environmentalist's favorite, "Endangered Species" list. When it was learned several tortoises had wandered into paths of big and powerful earth movers and crushed, the project had a big problem. So far that "turtle crisis" has cost the company building the project more than $56-million to protect and relocate tortoises whose habitat has been invaded by the sprawling Ivanpah solar project.

Desert tortoises are only one of Ivanpah's problems. Nine nearby military bases and the U.S. Defense Department have formally complained that the 45 story towers will generate a "heat source" that will interfere with the military's heat seeking missiles. In addition, navigation gear on jets could become jammed or receive inaccurate information.

The nearby Blythe Airport has also protested the construction project saying small planes accessing their airspace will fly over the giant solar plant producing superheated air. This can cause pilots to fly off course or encounter severe air turbulence resulting in possible crashes during take off and/or landings.

Then, there are the giant wind turbines. These are the industrial strength windmills that have received incredible amounts of government stimulus dollars. In Reno, Nevada seven giant wind turbines were built in 2010 at a cost of $1million in taxpayer dollars. When unveiled, the city said the new wind turbines would dramatically reduce the city's heating costs. So far, the city has saved a total of $2,785. Only naïve and green indoctrinated government bureaucrats could try to make sense of investing $1million to save a bit less than $3,000.

In the Altamont Pass of Northern California, 5,000 wind turbines cover the hillside. Each is seven stories tall with three blades that sweep an area the size of a football field at a rate of 20 times a minute. That means the blades spin at an amazing 200 feet per second. In the last 25 years, the giant windmills have become known as "giant bird killers". More than 7500 birds, including 67 Bald and Gold Eagles, have been killed by these large blades. Do you recall hearing or seeing anything about all of these deaths? Most of us know that since 1940, both the Bald and Golden Eagle have been protected by a federal act that bears their names as well as being listed on the Migratory Bird Act. For environmentalists not complaining about any of this is a bit hypocritical. But to date, no one has been prosecuted for any of the deaths; not under Presidents Obama, Bush or Clinton. Violators of the protection acts are supposed to be fined $5,000 for first time violations and/or one year in prison.

Apparently green energy projects are exempt from such penalties.

CHAPTER 8

CALIFORNIA GREEN DREAMIN'

In June of 2005, California Governor Arnold Schwartzen-housekeeper gave "a truly remarkable speech" at the World Environment Day (WED) Conference in San Francisco. Straying from President G.W. Bush's stance on global warming, Governor Arnold stated, "I say the debate is over. We know the science. We see the threat. And we know the time for action is now." Following his speech, the Governor signed **California Executive Order S-3-05** laying out a series of rules, regulations and target dates to reduce California's production of greenhouse gases. In 2006, Assembly Bill 32, the California "Global Warming Solutions Act of 2006", was written and introduced by California Speaker of the Assembly, Fabio Nunez. That same year the bill passed and was signed into law by Governor Arnold.

In light of the 'state of the state' and our nation today, it is interesting to reflect on the big World Environment Day event. Under the theme of Green Cities, the celebration went on for five days including topics such as Urban Power, Cities on the Move, Redesigning the Metropolis, Pure Elements, Flower Power and a Green Cities Expo.

Then U.N. Secretary-General, Kofi Annan, said, "It is most fitting that San Francisco, birthplace of the United Nations and one of the world's most dynamic urban areas, will be the host city for the global celebration of World Environment Day 2005."

As host city of the event, then Mayor Gavin Newsom said, "San Francisco is honored to host United Nations World Environment Day 2005. We are delighted to work with the United Nations Environment Program to make sure that World Environment Day in San Francisco leaves a legacy that will advance environmental well-being here at home and around the world".

Perhaps the most foreboding statement was made by then United Nations Environment Program (UNEP) Executive Director Klaus Toepfer who said, "It is up to cities in the developed world to set an example in areas such as the efficient use of energy and water. And it is incumbent upon them to partner developing world cities so they do not take a short-term 'dirty' development path, but a long-term sustainable one. If this can be done, we can help realize the UN Millennium Development Goals by 2015 and in doing so rid the world of poverty—the most toxic element of all."

Strangely, Assembly Bill 32 contained all three of the primary goals of the U.N.'s Agenda 21 as we outlined in Chapter 2. First, the identical greenhouse gases (GHG) listed in the U.N.1997 Kyoto Accords were copied gas by gas in AB 32. Next, the state's target for accomplishing control of CO-2 emissions was precisely the same as the goal in Agenda 21; roll back pollution levels to 1990 by the year 2020. Finally, and most destructive, California introduced its own version of the U.N.'s "Cap and Trade" scheme, omitting the global economic implications.

California's legislature assigned one state bureaucracy, the California Air Resources Board (CARB)—I like to refer to them as, California's Arbitrary Rules for Bankruptcy—the task of creating an economy-wide Cap and Trade program governing more than 400 businesses in the state. CARB was charged with developing "pollution caps" for each business. If violators exceeded their pollution caps, they were forced to purchase from the state "carbon credits", pieces of paper that essentially granted permission to continue polluting once they paid money to the state.

The strangling program took six years to design and was rolled out November 14, 2012.

Regretfully, California is no longer the "California Dream" I remember after moving here in the late 60s. Back then, in every measureable category, California was the most incredibly successful destination for families and businesses. With low humidity, average temperatures in the 70s and long, lazy, sunny days year 'round, aesthetically, the weather was—and still is—perfect.

The California school system was the envy of the nation. Schools were committed to graduating students who had an excellent chance of entering college, graduating and successfully contributing to society.

From 1969 through the 1990s, the California economy was the 6th largest in the world. Only five other nations on the planet had a larger domestic economy than California.

Business was thriving everywhere in the state. The space industry was headquartered here and later Silicon Valley, planted in the north part of the state, would transform the world of communications.

The entertainment industry was thriving; movie and television productions were booming and the global music business was humming. Who can forget the hit records of that era perfectly describing "California Dreamin" and, of course, the endless stream of Beach Boy classics that told the world about sunny, sandy beaches, cool ocean breezes and the laid back lifestyle of The Golden State.

California was home to the nation's aircraft and aerospace industry generating good paying jobs the year round. Living costs were relatively low, homes were affordable and the state government operated like a business with spending not grotesquely exceeding revenues.

That was then, this is now. Today, California is a disaster zone.

The state's economy hit the skids and sunk to 8th place in the world in less than a decade.

Businesses are fleeing from California at an alarming rate. Sadly, California has for the past four years received the dubious distinction by "CEO (Chief Executive Officer) Magazine" as "the state with the worst business climate in America".

There are now more California "tax takers" than "tax payers". Approximately one third of America's welfare recipients live in California and the state is home to a permanent welfare class. The poverty rate is above 23% of the state's total population.

Schools, if not already closed, are dangerous war zones in many communities. Others are in dire need of repairs and upgrades. Roads and bridges are dangerously in need of repair.

Income to the California State Franchise Board, the tax collecting agency, must total $6.4 billion per month if the state is to break even. For most months, $4 billion is being collected producing a monthly shortfall of nearly $2.5 billion. The state's bond rating is currently number 50 of the 50 states.

A liberal, one party, big government has taken over California. The state's giant political machine is supported by election donations from the state teachers union, large and well heeled environmental organizations, government employee's unions and, the notorious Service Employees International Union (SEIU) complete with their purple t-shirts. All contribute obscene amounts of money to get their hand-picked candidates elected to office.

Once elected, those hand-picked officials must negotiate work contracts with their allies whose lavish donations supported them, while the average state taxpayer is left to pay the bills. California now teeters precariously over its own fiscal cliff.

The Golden State leads the nation with the highest state sales and state income tax rates. Tiger Woods moved from California to Florida in 1996 because of his substantial tax burden. Florida has no state income tax. Golfer Phil Mickelson, a California native, recently admitted he was contemplating a similar move.

Officially, California's unemployment rate is listed a bit above 10%, but trade unions report among their members the number is more in the 20 to 40% range.

The space industry has long since closed up shop and departed. California's once-thriving boat manufacturing business is gone. Even Silicon Valley pioneers are relocating to other states and overseas. Doing business in California is simply too difficult.

Green is now the state's favorite color—"environmental green".

Environmentalism, through AB 32, cap and trade and the massive CARB bureaucracy, has foisted more environmental laws on the citizens and businesses of California than any other state in the nation. Faced with a "fight or flight" climate (either stay in California and fight the state's environmental laws or take flight and move operations elsewhere) businesses are running for the borders of Arizona, Nevada, and beyond.

In 2012, the Orange County Register newspaper reported that 254 California companies moved out of the state in 2011. That was 26% more than the previous year. Here are a few of the companies moving all, or some of their businesses and jobs, out of the state.

Thomas Brothers Maps moved to Skokie, Il. DirecTV closed operations in El Segundo and moved to Iowa. The Claim Jumper Restaurants and "Investor's Business Daily" relocated to Texas. Intel of Silicon Valley chose to build a new plant in Viet Nam.

Google built a beautiful new campus in Pittsburgh, PA., while Hyundai Capital America transferred 71 jobs to Georgia and Texas. EBay created 1,000 new jobs at a new plant in Austin, TX. Twitter and software giant Oracle are now headquartered in Salt Lake City. Apple built a new $304 million facility in TX creating 3600 jobs. Hilton Hotels, once the pride of Beverly Hills, moved to Virginia.

That long list of departed businesses is only a partial list of the hundreds that have fled the state. Demographer Joel Kotkin believes in 2013 the fastest growing business in California is "government" and the government's biggest product is "red tape".

In November, 2012 CARB implemented the draconian cap and trade program and conducted the first economy wide carbon credit auction in American history.

The California Chamber of Commerce called the complicated program "a job killer" and "an illegal tax" and filed a lawsuit to stop the auctions. The auction was held, but the case is still pending.

Phase one of the arbitrary CARB caps began on January 1, 2013, but were hardly mentioned by the state's mainstream media. As required by the AB 32 law, the complicated cap and trade scheme is being phased in over the next few years, about as slowly and imperceptibly as the global environmental movement has evolved in the last four decades. By the year 2015 when the final phase of the program slides into place, California's oil refineries will be responsible for all the emissions of the 27 million vehicles registered in the state.

There are only 14 oil refineries operating in the entire state of California to produce the gas at the pump needed by all those vehicles.

Refineries are currently ordered by the state to produce three different gas blends each year; a winter blend, a summer blend and now a new ethanol based, low carbon emitting fuel. That news sent oil investors surveying the future business climate in the state and some have already begun to pull their California plug.

British Petroleum put a for-sale sign on their huge refinery in Southern California. They have opted to invest in more profitable horizontal drilling operations in the great Pacific Northwest. An EXXON refinery in Northern California is considering the same course of action. Where will those 27million vehicles buy gas if oil refineries are exiting the state? Perhaps the drivers will be forced to park their vehicles and use public transportation (refer please to the chapters on the goals of Agenda 21 and ICLEI).

The New York Times analyzed California's cap and trade scheme and reported in a vast understatement of fact, "Opponents argue that it (cap and trade) would impose excessive costs in energy industries in a weak economy."

San Diego's Union newspaper called cap and trade an "initiative that will eventually affect Californians every time they take a shower, pump gas or watch TV". Yes, television. Using their unquestionable environmental wisdom, CARB has ruled that big screen TV's are a threat to the environment and must be tightly controlled.

For the first time in history, more people are leaving California than are moving here. The weather has stayed the same but the "climate" has certainly changed, especially for businesses.

The president of the San Francisco Small Business Network, Art Swanson, reports that in 2011 small business failures in California were 69% higher than the national average and California now claims 4 of the top 5 metropolitan areas in the nation for small business bankruptcies.

"Relocation Reps" are thriving in California. Other states now send representatives to California enticing businesses to relocate. "Move to our state," they say, "where there is no state income tax, we offer special incentives and will even provide you with a friendly government liaison to make your move go smoothly" (instead of an environmental bureaucracy with its hand out at every turn). Those from the other states remind business owners in California, "there is no Air Resources Board and there is no such thing as cap and trade".

Texas now tops the list of states where California businesses are relocating. Second is Arizona, third Nevada and Utah are tied, and Virginia and Oregon are tied for fourth.

How is the California state government reacting to the long list of business departures? Denial is the first response and disbelief is the second. Take for example the following exchange between a reporter and the California State Senate President, Darrell Steinberg.

Reporter: The Campbell Soup Company has operated here in Sacramento since 1947. It is the oldest of all of the company's soup plants across the country but it is closing down and laying off employees. Campbell says it costs more to produce a case of soup in Sacramento than at any of their other plants in America. Your response?

Steinberg (answering with a very broad smile): "Well, people aren't eating as much soup as they used to. And besides, the unemployed workers will get better union jobs."

Callous statements like that are not uncommon in a state that has been run by one political party for almost all of the last 30 years.

Consider for a moment how the California environmental bureaucracy has victimized the trucking industry. In 2007, CARB began to create their pollution caps and lots of new rules and regulations. They focused on truckers, declaring diesel trucks the state's worst polluters. CARB had a scientific study to support that claim.

Doctor Hein Tran, a graduate of the University of California at Davis and CARB science analyst, produced a study that was the basis for all of the onerous CARB air pollution regulations saddled onto California 's truckers.

He reported that in 2006, there were 3500 deaths recorded statewide directly attributable to "diesel particulate matter" inhaled by unsuspecting citizens. Those citizen-victims demanded the government's environmental protection.

Many wondered how Dr. Tran arrived at such a shocking number of deaths caused by diesel truck emissions. Were there autopsy reports that listed the cause of death as "the inhalation of diesel particulate matter"? Logical questions aside, Dr. Tran's report was accepted and approved by the state's environmental board. Based on Dr. Tran's scientific research, a long list of stringent trucking regulations was officially passed by CARB in December of 2007.

One regulation stipulated a truck more than 7 years old must be replaced. CARB claimed older trucks caused pollution, ignoring the fact that the replacement of a single truck could cost an operator as much as $130,000. If a business owns a fleet of usable but aging trucks, say 20, replacing them would cost the company $26-million. CARB also demanded a truck, newer than seven years old, must be retrofitted at cost about $15,000 per truck. Astounding, indeed.

Just as the regulations were about to be passed into law, a large scandal erupted that was nick-named "Trangate" in honor of Dr. Tran. Investigative journalists began reviewing his resume and what they found was shocking.

Tran wasn't really a PhD graduate of UC Davis. In fact, he received his advanced degree, not from UCD, but from UPS. Tran's diploma was ordered on-line from a London "diploma mill" Thornhill University. For a few extra dollars, Tran also received the distinction of "Magna Cum Laude".

In the summer of 2007, the revelation of Tran's phony doctorate combined with the outrageous claims made in his research study was sent to the director of CARB, Mary Nichols. She reviewed them and decided to keep the report under lock and key until all of the onerous "diesel particulate matter" rules were passed and put into effect. Then she revealed the incredible deception of the "Trangate" scandal to the members of her Board.

Was severe disciplinary action taken against Dr. Tran? Far from being fired, after the shocking revelation of fraud and deception were made public, Dr. Tran was given a monthly pay raise of $1,006. As of 2012, he is still on CARB's payroll at an annual salary of $87,492.52.

Such is the way of California environmental law implementation in the first decade of the new millennium.

The thrust of California's incredible litany of eco-babble rules, regulations, and the cap and trade scheme can be traced back to Agenda 21 and the 1997 Kyoto Accords. And now, through the ICLEI's intrusion some of the state's largest metropolitan areas and regional planning boards are adopting the U.N.'s Green Agenda and bypassing locally elected officials.

Earlier, I referred to the 1997 founding of the "Bay Area Alliance for Sustainable Communities" shortly after the U.N.'s Kyoto Accords were compiled into Agenda 21. Here is the quote of that group's mission statement. "The Bay Area Alliance adopted the definition of sustainable development endorsed by the United Nation's World Commission on Environment and Development. The Earth Charter Initiative is an outgrowth of the 1992 Earth Summit in Rio de Janeiro and has many principals similar to the opinions and commitments contained in this Compact."

Nine counties that include 66 independent cities are under the One Bay Area banner and have created a regional planning program that is unlike any other in the state. In the 15 years since it began its work, the organization has proposed projects ranging from an ambitious web of bike paths to new and improved public transportation corridors complete with "stack and pack" affordable housing projects that are all within easy walking distance of transit stops, just as Agenda 21 and ICLEI suggested. Now, as local citizens of those 9 counties and 66 cities are becoming informed about the origins and goals of One Bay Area, public hearings are becoming downright contentious and rebellion is in the air.

Up and down the state 136 California cities have already signed up to be recognized as ICLEI Gold Star communities and all have dutifully paid their dues to the United Nations. The massive, complicated and heavy handed UN Agenda 21 is probably already operating through a regional planning organization in your community. Under the guise of stopping global warming, ICLEI organizations are popping up everywhere like mushrooms in the night.

The forty year skid from "California Dreamin'" to "California Disaster" is a cautionary tale for the rest of America. An old adage proclaims, "As California goes, so goes the nation." The cautionary tale is if the U.N. ICLEI agenda has gained such a strong foothold in California and has become an economic disaster here, citizens across America—beware.

As President Obama outlined in his 2013 State of the Union address, cap and trade or a carbon tax, along with other draconian regulations may be enforced by the unelected and virtually autonomous—EPA. As all of the anecdotal evidence from California demonstrates, over zealous eco-babble regulations are never good medicine for a sick economy.

The terms "sustainable", global warming, and GHG's translate as they have in California, into imaginary pollution controls with questionable deadlines. If allowed to continue, a "green tsunami" will sweep across America and ultimately destroy this once great country.

Incidentally, as this book goes to press, President Obama's Secretary of the Environmental Protection Agency, Lisa Jackson, has resigned her post. Among the names being floated as her replacement is none other than California CARB director, Mary Nichols. Remember that name. As we have mentioned, Nichols has single handedly presided over the implementation of AB 32 complete with cap and trade. When mentioning Nichols in his publication, "Daily Caller", Tucker Carlson called her "the most dangerous woman in America". Considering her competition, that is a shocking achievement.

Nichols is a lifelong environmental activist and attorney. She filed the very first successful lawsuit under President Nixon's 1972 Clean Air Act. Her victory in that case made her the "poster girl" of the early days of neo-environmentalism. She was a founding attorney for the Los Angeles office of the powerful environmental law group mentioned earlier, NRDC. She accepted her first state environmental appointment in the 70s, during Governor Jerry Brown's first term in office. When Brown departed, Nichols was named the first environmental officer hired by the city of Los Angeles. In her new post, she developed a penchant for politics and became the director of L.A.'s then-mayor, Tom Bradley, as he campaigned to be the first black governor of California. When Bradley lost the election, Nichols taught environmental law at UCLA, the same school where Al Gore's power point talk was "discovered" by the Hollywood elite.

Nichols is described in her official state biography as "responsible for implementing California's tough new vehicle emissions standards which are stricter than federal requirements and aim to reduce emissions from cars and light trucks by 30% by 2016."

If Nichols replaces Jackson in the second term of the Obama Administration, reread this chapter very thoroughly and be reminded how this unelected official with virtually no oversight of her massive CARB bureaucracy has destroyed California's economy. Imagine for a moment California's disaster, on steroids, being implemented across the United States. Then you must decide whether her path of globalist environmentalism is the best path for America's future.

Our dots are collected and connected. Now what do you do with them? Read on.

CHAPTER 9

STOP THE "GREEN TSUNAMI": YOUR PERSONAL 'TO DO' LIST

Unlike a natural tidal wave, the "Green Tsunami" can be stopped before it becomes a national catastrophe of epic proportion. But to accomplish the goal of reversing public opinion and political will, we must all become actively involved.

Quite honestly, most of us feel impotent when the subject involves matters of national or international politics. The United Nations and the list of capitols around the world where U.N. offices work every day to push their global agenda seem far, far out of our reach.

But the U.N. depends for its operating budget on American tax dollars. Without Uncle Stupid picking up a huge portion of the globalist's tab, the U.N. building in New York City would fetch a hefty selling price from "The Donald". He would no doubt convert it into lovely condos or offices overlooking the magnificent East River.

So first things first, we must launch a nationwide campaign to stop funding the U.N.

Consider yourself a committee of one and please start calling, writing and e-mailing your three congressional representatives (two U.S.

Senators and the Congressman/woman) who represent your district. To find their names and contact information, click onto "Congress. org" and enter your zip code and mailing address into the system. Some Congressional Districts are split within a single zip code so your address is a very important entry.

Pictures of your two Senators and Congress person will appear on your computer screen along with the leaders of both the House and the Senate. Notice too, if you click onto "Advocacy 101" and the tab "Communicating with Congress", you get helpful, practical suggestions about contacting your representatives. You can compose one single, very brief letter and with one click of your mouse your comments are sent to ALL of your Federal lawmakers.

Second, begin to spread the word about Agenda 21, ICLEI and America's participation in the United Nation's Agenda 21 program. Talk with your neighbors, your friends, your co-workers and ask them to join your campaign. Ask your U.S. Congressman and Senator to support H.R. 75 without delay and "get us out of the U.N. and the U.N. out of America". Tell them we need those billions of dollars invested every year into the U.N.'s global governance scheme brought back home to America so we can improve our schools, fix our roads, hire police and firemen and not pay for the advancement of a the globalist/environmental agenda.

Remember, your government representatives work for YOU and you have a right to their time. Ask for a 15 minute appointment and visit them when they are home from D.C. and in their district office. Make your voice heard, get active and save America.

The third action item is to do some investigative work and find out if your local community is promoting "Agenda 21" through ICLEI. Many states now link the distribution of highway funds and transportation dollars to the goals of the U.N. and ICLEI. **If your city is already an ICLEI "Gold Star" city, get busy.** Make an appointment to visit with your local government officials. Ask if they know about Agenda 21 and the way globalists are attempting to use environmental issues to establish their New World Order through ICLEI. Whether their answer is "yes" or "no", discuss it with them. You may have some information to share with them that they knew little or nothing about.

Take a copy of this book with you and ask them to read it. Then, make a follow-up appointment to discuss the book and any state programs that are implementing this expensive and subversive U.N. agenda. Remember, environmentalism is constructed on a bedrock of half truths and untruths that scientists everywhere are now disputing.

Speak at city council meetings, write letters to your local newspapers and call local talk radio programs. Consider the impact you as a citizen can have on your local community. Has the U.N. globalism/socialist agenda, originally articulated by Dr. Bruntland in the 1980s, compiled into Agenda 21 by Bruntland and Strong in the 90s and promoted by Al Gore in the last decade invaded your hometown? Have well meaning local politicians bought into the discredited environmental agenda of the last century? Is your city's planning department, not realizing that the goals of the U.N.'s plans to supersede representative government are bringing this scheme to your hometown?

To be really encouraged, go to the website The Oregon Project. You will be shocked by the growing list of scientists who are publicly expressing skepticism about the claims of environmental alarmism. In 1997 when the Kyoto Accords were compiled into Agenda 21, a handful of scientists developed "The Oregon Project Global Warming Petition" and began signing it. It has spread like a California wild fire. When last I checked, a total of 31,487 scientists have added their signatures to the statement, "There is no credible evidence between man-made pollution and global warming." 9,029 of the scientists are PhD's, real PhD's.

Fourth, you need to get educated and stay educated so you can address this complex issue thoroughly, honestly and unemotionally. The other side is continually adding new elements or upgrading old ones to their eco-babble. Arm yourself with truth—it wins every time.

One great source of information is the Principal Research Scientist at the University of Alabama, Huntsville, Dr. Fred Singer. He is also the U.S. Team Leader for the advance microwave scanning radiometer aboard NASA's Aqua Satellites. In July of 2012, Dr. Singer issued a report that says in part; "According to data collected from 2000 to 2011 the Earth's Atmosphere is allowing more heat to be released into space than computer-generated models predicted." In other words, computers are great for family fun, for school projects and for creating unbelievable special effects for Hollywood movies, but no computer program can predict the complexities of how the Universe will function for the next century. If we learned any lesson from the Climategate fiasco, computers are only as reliable as the information we feed into them.

Also, my radio pal, Brian Sussman, certified meteorologist and former TV weatherman in San Francisco, now host of a top rated conservative radio talk show, has written two great books on the subject of environmentalism and Agenda 21; "Climategate" and "Eco Tyranny", respectively. In chapter twelve of his latest book, he writes, "The year is 2050"… he goes on to imagine what life would be like if the environmentalists have their way and control the way we live. It is hilarious reading complete with a description of the local "Office of Green Living" that advises future citizens to subscribe to the three-R's—reuse, reduce and recycle. Small is better in the world of global environmentalism, where a chosen few elitists will make lifestyle choices for the rest of us. The New World Order that Sussman describes is a world more suited to a science fiction movie like "Soylent Green" but it is hardly the kind of world we would all like to leave behind for our children and future generations.

If your government officials have been unresponsive to your requests, start a petition drive in your city. (**Remember, when elected officials feel the heat, invariably they see the light.**) Tom DeWeese is leading the charge in the state of Virginia. Click on to "VAright" (Virginia Right) for a sample petition, then duplicate it adapting it to your local community. Circulate the petition; ask your friends, neighbors and family members to help you gather signatures. Keep the media informed about your campaign and its progress.

Invite your family, neighbors and friends to your home for coffee and desert and have a discussion about environmentalism and the far reaching tentacles of "Agenda 21". I met Ben Stein at his house in Malibu some time ago and he called environmentalism "the biggest threat to America behind only Islamic terrorism". Be prepared to confront the parts of "Agenda 21" that others might embrace. Be "firm, frank, fair and friendly" as you expose the history of the environmental movement going back to Earth Day 1970 and bring them forward from there using nothing more than facts and common sense.

By the way, another wonderful source for truthful up to the minute environmental reporting is the website *www.climatedepot.com*, (think of Climate Depot as the Home Depot of climate information). It is maintained by Mark Morano, once staffer for Senator James Inhofe of Oklahoma when he chaired the Senate Committee on Environmental Issues. Through this experience, Mark became an expert on environmental issues. More and more, he is gaining national exposure especially on the Fox News Network and CNN commenting on breaking environmental news stories. His website is absolutely without peer.

Climate Depot is a part of a longtime Washington environmental truth telling organization, the Committee for a Constructive Tomorrow. For 28 years, the co-founders of CFACT, Craig Rucker and David Rothbard, have been trekking all over the planet attending U.N. climate meetings. They are not only an outstanding news and information source, but I admire them for their creative activism and why my wife and I worked with them in 2008 to stop Cap and Trade nationally. In 2009, CFACT actually boarded a Greenpeace ship in the Copenhagen harbor where a U.N. climate conference was being held. Once onboard, they unfurled a large banner over the existing Greenpeace banner "The Rainbow Warrior" that now read "Propaganda Warrior" and the CFACT name. For four decades, I have heard of Greenpeace members boarding other ships; but not until 2009 had I heard of their ship being "boarded".

The best source for ICLEI information is the ICLEI website itself. They make no secret about their U.N. affiliation, about their globalist goals and about their strategy to take the world from where we are now to where they want the world to be; a world of urban hubs, public transportation, shortages of electric power and water and Smart Meters. They forthrightly describe their goals of creating a centralized bureaucracy that can monitor your family's utility use and if you exceed your government ordered caps, those Smart Meters will activate and reduce your power use by remote control.

By the way, if Smart Meter technology isn't already on your eco-babble radar screen, you can learn about not only Smart Meters, but also the Smart Grid and the new Smart Appliances that are being designed for your home and workplace. Google the words "smart meters" to find out what that new digital electric meter that has been installed on your property, most likely without your permission, is designed to accomplish. A detailed study of Smart Meters is provided in the timely new book, "Just Say No To Smart Meters" by Orlean Koehle, California president of the Eagle Forum.

One area I did not get into was education. Yes, folks, they are going after our education system too and must be stopped. A former teacher herself, Orlean has also written, "Common Core"—A Trojan Horse for Education Reform that goes into terrific detail concerning yet another global tentacle.

There is not a rock you can turn over that these globalists have not already been working under.

Let me close by being frank. Global Environmentalism and Global Governance has leaped out of the starting blocks and has a huge lead in the race to create their New World Order. For nearly half a century, they have been imposing their propaganda like the old Chinese "water torture"—drip, drip, drip. No matter how hard we try, we are not going to turn public opinion around in one week, one month, one year, one election or perhaps one decade. But we can and we must begin—now—today.

Remember the words of the great American patriot Andrew Jackson, the 7th President of our great nation. "Providence," he said, "has showered on this favored land, blessings without number. And He has chosen you as the guardians of freedom—to preserve it for the benefit of the human race. May He, who holds in His hands the destinies of the nations, make you worthy of the favors He has bestowed among you."

And please remember a final bit of ancient wisdom: "The journey of a thousand miles begins with a single step".

CHAPTER 10

LATE BREAKING
ENVIRONMENTAL NEWS UPDATES

As a final update, here are a few miscellaneous late-breaking news tidbits you need to know:

The U.N.'s notorious IPCC that was discredited during the Climategate Scandal is at it again. The Climate Research Group is about to issue an updated report on Climate Change, Global Warming and Greenhouse Gases. Who will provide the "expert science" for their 2013 study? Nine of the studies were done in whole, or in part, by The World Wildlife Fund (WWF), another of the long list of mega-international environmental organizations. The WWF, you will recall, produced the panic about the Himalayan Glaciers melting by 2035. Two WWF employees and other activist environmentalists will serve as "scientific reviewers" of the new IPCC study. Be forewarned. The new U.N. report will most likely be another round of eco-babble written from a globalist Agenda 21 perspective.

California's industrial emission of green house gases dropped for the third year in a row. This was before the Draconian AB 32 laws were implemented and before the state's Cap and Trade auctions began. Stated simply, without the state's stringent environmental laws ordered by the unelected members of the California Air Resources Board, businesses around the state are already reducing air pollution to 1992 levels, but it didn't taken them to the year 2020.

The California Air Resources Board is levying expensive fines on the state's businesses that fail to comply with their AB 32 rules and regulations. Foster Enterprises was slapped with a $300,000 fine after CARB said they failed to upgrade their refrigerated diesel trailer fleet (review Chapter 8 for CARB's diesel truck regulations). One reporter wrote, "In Texas, the officials welcome business. But in California the state government sends out press releases celebrating the massive fines they impose on private enterprise". By the way, Foster Enterprises is not a part of Foster Farms, the chicken folks.

California's governor, a majority of his state legislators and his "deep pocket" environmental buddies continue to push for approval of a public transportation fiasco "The Bullet Train to Nowhere". In 2008, the massive high speed rail project was introduced to California voters as Prop 1A. Voters were told the $10 billion project would deliver passengers from San Francisco to Los Angeles in two hours and forty minutes and the entire project would be completed in 2020. The project has been in the works for five years without a shovel of dirt being turned and the estimated cost ballooning to nearly $100 billion.

Recently, Governor Brown revised the costs downward and now estimates the completed project will cost only $68 billion. The completion date is now 2028, if not a single lawsuit is filed to delay construction. That amazing amount of spending would set a new record for "the fastest rate of construction in U.S. transportation history". In Governor Brown's revised plan, the bullet train passes through major cities but shares tracks with Amtrak and other slower moving trains. In order to launch his massive boondoggle, state officials must obtain 120 individual land use permits and purchase 1,100 parcels of land (most of it, prime Central Valley farm land). Potential bullet train customers say, faced with a choice between the proposed plans for the "slow-speed" bullet train and a commuter airline, they would choose the more convenient, less expensive plane ticket from

L.A. to San Francisco, with a one way travel time of approximately 70 minutes.

Hurricane Sandy is, according to President Obama, Al Gore and other green activists, an obvious example of climate change producing intense storms that destroy America's low lying coastal communities. In the wake of Hurricane Sandy, Al Gore said, "…. Sandy is a disturbing sign of things to come. We must heed this warning and act quickly to solve the climate crisis. Dirty energy makes dirty weather". Environmental experts report the exact opposite is true. As bad as Hurricane Sandy was, it is not considered to have been, in technical terms, a major hurricane. In fact, the United States has now set a record of more than 2,500 days without being struck by a Category 3 or larger hurricane. Since 1950, hurricane strikes in Florida have been progressively further apart.

America's deadliest hurricane happened in 1900 long before our industrial revolution began causing pollution that is supposedly to blame for "Climate Change". In short, scientists and historians tell us a completely different tale than the climate alarmists and their political and media allies. There is no conceivable connection between Hurricane Sandy and "Climate Change", no matter what President Obama and his new Secretary of State, John Kerry, might claim.

In another late breaking news story, Warren Buffett and a division of his Berkshire-Hathaway conglomerate is now the second largest solar operator in America. Does that mean that solar power is a top grade investment for you to add to your portfolio? Michael Horowitz in the Financial Times analyzed the report and suggested that under the latest version of the Congress "avoiding the fiscal cliff deal" taxpayers will continue to subsidize green developers with an incredible 30% of their total projected costs in cash. The Sage of Omaha is merely tapping into a river of never-ending government venture capital for gigantic solar experiments. California for example, demands that 33% of all of the state's electricity must come from renewable sources by 2020. Twenty nine other states are making similar demands. Buffet has simply made another very shrewd investment and America's taxpayers will contribute to his bottom line profits for the foreseeable green future.

California is now known as "The Saudi Arabia of Natural Gas". An untapped shale oil deposit, The Monterrey Field stretches from the Pacific Coast to the inland community of Bakersfield. That translates into California sitting atop a 200 mile wide ocean of untapped oil. The U.S. Energy Information Agency says the deposit contains an unimaginable 15.4 billion barrels of oil which is almost the total of all of America's conventional oil reserves. In dollars, if California were to join Texas, Alaska and North Dakota and open the Monterrey field for development, the economic benefit would exceed a staggering $1trillion. California would become one of the major exporters of oil in the world. To economically mine the oil in the Monterrey field, developers would use the horizontal drilling method known as "fracking". (The technique opposed by radical environmentalists who were willing to show their protest by handcuffing themselves to the fence surrounding the White House.) Of course, California's radical environmentalists have fallen in step to oppose "fracking" in California as well. While Governor Brown constructs his latest budget based on new taxes, California could be awash in billions of new natural profits and leasing revenues, if only....

EPILOGUE

And now, here is a personal addition to this book that I would like to leave with you.

I am a Christian.

I believe, God created the Earth. I believe that simple statement is at the very heart of the Global Environmentalism debate. There are those who believe the earth and the universe came into existence by a "Big Bang" that happened eons ago. But they never seem to be able to answer the simple question, who made the stuff that went bang?

I believe, everything we see around us is the work of a marvelous Creator. Stated another way, if we see a beautiful building, somewhere there is an architect who designed it. If there is a painting to be appreciated, somewhere there is a painter.

The entire universe around us functions so perfectly, so minutely and intricately perfect, that it begs for a simple yet fundamental question, "Did it all happen by accident and did man evolve from a single cell and suddenly become Bill Gates?

Frankly, I don't have enough faith to be an atheist. It is much easier for me to simply acknowledge that there is a Creator who I call God, the Father, and He rules the universe He created—and quite frankly, doesn't need my help.

I believe there are fundamental laws that operate behind this marvelous creation. No one invented the Law of Gravity—it existed before mankind was smart enough to recognize and codify it. The same holds true for the Laws of Centrifugal Force, Relativity and Curved Space. Whether you believe in God or not, those laws apply to all of us.

If two people leap from the San Francisco Bay Bridge and one of them believes in God and the other doesn't, they will both hit the water at the exact same time. The Law of Gravity, created by God who designed this universe, prevails.

By the way, the God I have come to know is perfectly capable of maintaining His creation. The planets will continue to revolve around the Sun and any other Suns and Universes we have yet to discover. God is keeping them operating too.

The earth is at the precise, perfect distance from the Sun so life can exist. If we were a few degrees off in our orbit through the Universe, the earth would be too hot or too cold for life to survive.

Can mankind screw up those fundamental rules that keep the earth and the universe functioning? I don't think so. Honestly, I do not think the flatulence of farm animals, the exhaust from a tailpipe or the eco-babble we hear around us will seriously hamper the functioning of the universe. The assurance I maintain is that Creation and life will come to an end when the Creator decides it will and not a nanosecond sooner or later.

My wife and I once spent an afternoon with one of the NASA astronauts who walked on the moon. Imagine that reality. And yet with all of his scientific knowledge and all his critical thinking, he does not believe in a Creator or God. While I find that remarkable, everyone is entitled to their belief.

If you believe creation was an accident and that mankind simply evolved out of a simple one cell creature, you are still confronted with the question, who created that one cell creature?

Either God has everything under His control or He doesn't. And further, if He doesn't and He needs my help, we're all in trouble. Quite honestly, I don't spend much time each day thinking about the orbit of the earth.

Nor do I think to myself each day, "That was a monstrous breakfast this morning, I'm really going to need to manufacture lots of extra digestive fluids today." Or, "I'm going to sleep now, so I have to put my heart on automatic control so it keeps beating, my lungs continue to filter air and my blood keeps flowing." Each night, by faith, I go to sleep and don't worry about my body's functions for the next eight or nine hours.

I live each day expecting to live tomorrow and lots of tomorrows. Perhaps that is hope. I call it faith. I voluntarily chose to put my faith in the God who created me—that He will sustain me on His earth and in His universe until the day He decides it will end. Believe me, having arrived at that point in my life gives me great peace.

I recommend that you think Faith through. How did the Earth begin? Was it created or is everything around you an accident? If it was created, does it have rules we can discover? Albert Einstein once asked, "Do you live in a hostile or friendly universe?" Am I at peace with the world around me and with my fellow humans and all of the creation I see?

If I were troubled and not at peace, I would hope to keep my unrest to myself and not pollute (pardon the pun) the world around me with my suspicions and paranoia.

I believe we can all do more to live a life that overflows with peace and caring for others. I don't need orders from any political or military government demanding that I be more caring. I have discovered the wonders of charitable giving on my own. A concept that the government must take from the rich and redistribute to the poor calling it "social justice" or any other name is coercive, government-demanded-charity. It is a curse, not a blessing.

And I believe we must all learn to once again respect each other. That doesn't mean you must think a certain way, live a certain way or believe a certain way that agrees, totally, with me. But you must permit me to have my opinion and I will do the same for you.

If you honestly don't believe there is a creator that is fine. But please don't impose your way of thinking on me. Give me the freedom and respect to believe the way I want. I promise, I will do the same for you.

Harmony is a wonderful thing and I believe God created it too. To make musical harmony, each instrument or voice adds one note to create a chord. Harmonious chords are always beautiful to hear but if one note is slightly off key, there is a discord and it sounds shrill. Do we want to create a world of harmony and beauty—or a world of discord and ugliness?

Paraphrasing the remarkable G K Chesterton; harmony isn't something that we have tried and it has failed us; harmony is something we have tried, found difficult to achieve and simply discarded it.

Hopefully, the discord that the Global Environmental Movement has created will quickly fade away so the rest of us can learn to live harmoniously—and freely—on a planet that isn't hostile to any of us.

My astronaut friend told me when he was traveling through space that the Earth appeared through his porthole as a beautiful blue planet, silently orbiting the earth. Once he got to the moon, the earth was precisely in its place in orbit so he and his team could head the space craft back home and land safely.

The color of Earth isn't green—unless that giant Green Tsunami is allowed to sweep across the planet and cause global governance to reign supreme and cause individual freedom and liberty to become extinct.

Would that such a day would never happen.

INFORMATION SOURCES

Friends for Saving California Jobs—friendsforcajobs.com The more information my wife and I discovered concerning the globalist roots of radical environmentalism in California and its harm on the state and economy, there was no doubt we had to take action. We recruited three friends/businessmen Robert Ming , Bill Dunlap , Eric Eisenhammer, as well as a selection of prominent businessmen and women throughout the state to assist in our efforts to stop the out of control burdensome regulations strangling California companies. Visit our website to learn more about our team, join our coalition and stay up-to-date with the latest issues and actions you can take to make a difference in your state and the nation.

Climatedepot.com—regularly updated environmental news from Marc Morano, a longtime D.C. insider on environmental issues.

"The Greatest Hoax"—How the Global Warming Conspiracy Threatens Your Future—is Senator Jim Inhofe's detailed insider account of global environmentalism as he occupied a courtside seat observing how environmentalism works within our government to control the lives of every American in DC. His book is recommended by former Apollo 17 astronaut Harrison Schmitt, who is also a former U.S. Senator. This book is also available from WNDbooks.com.

CFACT.com—Website for the 28-year old environmental truth-telling organization, CFACT. Co-founders, David Rothbard and Craig Rucker have traveled millions of miles pursuing the truth on anthropologic (man-made) global warming.

CFACTSoCal.org—The website my wife and I started two years ago after establishing a state chapter office of CFACT. Our site is complete with lots of environmental news, speaking schedules, and recommended sources.

John Coleman—John is the weatherman at San Diego station KUSI and founder of the Weather Channel. Now this guy is a wonderful man and someone who really knows about weather! Go to KUSI. com and click on John's personal webpage, "Coleman's Corner"— This Webpage is Devoted to My Effort to Debunk the Alarmism of Global Warming... couldn't have said it better, friend!

Wattsuwiththat.com—California meteorologist Anthony Watts launched this website in 2006 just as the California Global Warming Solutions Act was coming to fruition. Check it out daily. It is the "most viewed website on global warming and climate change in the world".

drroyspencer.com—Dr. Spencer served as the Senior Scientist for Climate Studies at NASA's Marshall Space Center and is a self described environmental alarmism skeptic. His undergraduate degree is in Atmospheric Sciences and his two advanced degrees were both earned at the University of Wisconsin-Madison.

CalWatchdog.org—A great independent website sponsored by the Pacific Research Institute. Many of my state environmental articles are published at this site along with the great work of investigative journalist Katie Grimes.

Coalitionofenergyusers.org—Founder Eric Eisenhammer created a nonprofit grassroots movement dedicated to expanding access to affordable energy and quality jobs. Visit this website for all breaking California environmental news.

Environmental Perspectives—Google the organization's name and you'll meet the man who single-handedly stopped a US Senate vote on the UN's Biodiversity Treaty in 1994, Dr. Michael Coffman. His Doctorate in Forrest Sciences makes him a great source for "environmental perspectives". His outstanding books are available at his

EPI website.

Brian Sussman—San Francisco talk show host and former TV weatherman who has written two great books I highly recommend. "Climategate"—A Veteran Meteorologist Exposes the Global Warming Scam. And his follow-up, "Eco-Tyranny"—How the Left's Green Agenda Will Dismantle America. On the front cover of "Eco-Tyranny" is a wonderful endorsement from Senator James Inhofe. Both books can be ordered through the WorldNet Daily website, wndbooks.com.

ICLEI.org—Nothing like getting educated about this UN organization directly from their own website. ICLEI makes no secret of their history, their goals and their campaigns. Check to see if your hometown is an "ICLEI GOLD STAR" city.

Agenda 21—Your search engine will provide you with a wealth of information about the UN's Agenda for the 21st Century, along with the history of the organization, its founders and how it is positioned to advance a New World Order in the 21st century.

Jamesdelingpole.com—The website of the English investigative journalist who was one of the first to break the UN's IPCC Climategate Scandal wide open. He details the emails and reports all of the characters involved in the scheme by name. His book reveals what we all suspect about radical environmentalists: they are green on the outside but pink in the middle. Thus, his book is titled "Watermelon" and is available from watermelonsbook.com. Read his book.

SPPI.org/Monckton—Another Englishman has written several great books and is a constant source of updated climate information analysis. Lord Christopher Monckton is the Third Viscount of Benchley and was Lady Margaret Thatcher's advisor on environmental issues in the 1980s. His investigative research is available at the Science and Public Policy Institute website. He is a real-life genius who retains a marvelous sense of humor. SPPI is a not-for-profit institute of research and education dedicated to sound public policy based on sound science.

"Power Grab" by Chris Horner. Subtitled, "How Obama's green policies will steal your freedom and bankrupt America". Talk show host Mark Levin says the book "exposes the agenda of the Obama Administration and its allies" and it is also endorsed by Congresswoman

Michelle Bachman, a personal hero of mine.

"Imprimis" is the powerful monthly pamphlet publication from Hillsdale College in Michigan, a school based on a classical liberal arts model. Subscription is free at imprimis@hillsdale.edu

WND.com—Joe Farrahs' brash website, worldnetdaily.com is a powder keg of news and information unreported by the mainstream media. It is one of the most widely read news websites in the world.

American Values—This organization was founded by Gary Bauer and is a longtime favorite. Gary started the organization Family Research Council and served in the Reagan White House. His daily end of the day report from the Nation's Capitol provides you with lots of information and insights you need to know.

Refusesmartmeters.com—This book didn't give extensive coverage to the Smart Meters being installed on homes all over America and usually without the homeowner's permission. This website provides the most comprehensive information.

NOTES

NOTES

NOTES

NOTES